POT-BELLIED PIGS
AS A FAMILY PET
TS-188

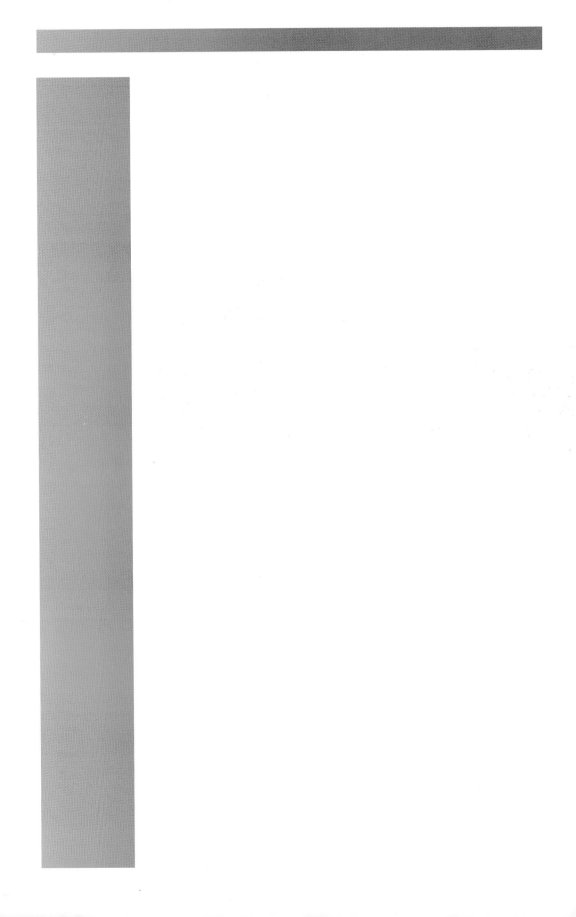

POT-BELLIED PIGS
AS A FAMILY PET

MICHAEL TAYLOR

Distributed in the UNITED STATES to the Pet Trade by T.F.H. Publica-
tions, Inc., One T.F.H. Plaza, Neptune City, NJ 07753; distributed in the
UNITED STATES to the Bookstore and Library Trade by National Book
Network, Inc. 4720 Boston Way, Lanham MD 20706; in CANADA to the
Pet Trade by H & L Pet Supplies Inc., 27 Kingston Crescent, Kitchener,
Ontario N2B 2T6; Rolf C. Hagen Ltd., 3225 Sartelon Street, Montreal
382 Quebec; in CANADA to the Book Trade by Macmillan of Canada (A
Division of Canada Publishing Corporation), 164 Commander Boule-
vard, Agincourt, Ontario M1S 3C7; in ENGLAND by T.F.H. Publications,
PO Box 15, Waterlooville PO7 6BQ; in AUSTRALIA AND THE SOUTH
PACIFIC by T.F.H. (Australia), Pty. Ltd., Box 149, Brookvale 2100
N.S.W., Australia; in NEW ZEALAND by Brooklands Aquarium Ltd., 5
McGiven Drive, New Plymouth, RD1 New Zealand; in the PHILIPPINES
by Bio-Research, 5 Lippay Street, San Lorenzo Village, Makati, Rizal;
in SOUTH AFRICA by Multipet Pty. Ltd., P.O. Box 35347, Northway,
4065, South Africa. Published by T.F.H. Publications, Inc. Manufac-
tured in the United States of America by T.F.H. Publications, Inc.

Contents

Acknowledgments

Special thanks go to Joann Webster and Linda Pryor, whose love and affection for these porcine pets knows no bounds and whose piggies appear in this book, and to William P. Rives, V.M.D. for making a very special house call.

Photography: Isabelle Français, Michael Gilroy, Vince Serbin, and Joann Webster.

Introduction

If there is one thing we humans cannot be accused of, it is displaying a lack of variety in the pet animals with which we choose to share our homes. Within any locality, you will, of course, see dogs, cats, rabbits and hamsters. You will most certainly find parrots and other birds, as well as a multitude of fishes in various forms. Over the years, a number of monkey species have caught our imagination. Currently, the most rapidly rising group of creatures that we find most fascinating is that of reptiles: snakes and lizards. But what about a pig in your bed!

That's right, a pig, and in particular a pot-bellied pig, the most expensive chunk of bacon you will find anywhere at this time. While there have always been those who have found the regular domestic pig to be a fascinating animal, to the degree that many have been kept as pets, these pigs have rarely enjoyed in-home status. Not so the pot-belly, which has taken the pet scene by storm in the last few years. These pint-sized porkers are now found in thousands of homes and enjoy the same privileges that in the past have been accorded to only the most regal of pets: cats and dogs.

In a pot-belly home, you will find them reclining near the fireside or on the laps of their devoted owners. They will be seen playing with cats and dogs, and come bedtime many will be found stretched out on the bedclothes—sandwiched between their loving owners. Yes, a pig in the bed really is true!

When you look at a baby pot-belly you can understand why people take so readily to them, but by the time they are fully grown they do have a look about them that only the most loving of mothers could find beautiful. Of course, beauty is in the eye of the beholder, but by no

Opposite: A pot-bellied pig foraging for edibles. Pigs are omnivorous, which is one of the reasons why they originally came to be kept as household livestock: they could easily be fattened on scraps left over from the family dinner.

stretch of the imagination could you say the pot-belly is gorgeous. Clearly then, it must have something else going for it. And so it has. Through selective breeding and adhering to show standards, breeders have been able to maintain the short nose, cobby body, and lovable personality characteristic of the pot-belly. Indeed, there are many virtues that make this porcine pet a delightful animal to have around the home. By the time you have read this book it is hoped that you will appreciate the qualities that thousands of people over the centuries have recognized in members of the genus *Sus*.

However, the fact that the pot-belly has rocketed to pet stardom does not mean it is suited to every home. It presents a number of practical problems, including one that involves its status, or not, as a pet, depending on the locality in which you live. Although a common everyday animal, the pot-bellied pig is presently still within that group of pets that some people think of as "exotic."

If you own a dog, cat, bird, or rabbit, the chances are you have some basic understanding about how to care for it, but not so the pig. What does it eat? How big will it grow? Can it be trained? What illnesses can it get? These questions and many others need to be answered before you venture out to purchase this unusual pet. Then there is the matter of where you should obtain a pot-belly from and how to judge whether or not it is both a healthy specimen and genuine. The dramatic rise in popularity of these miniature pigs, hogs, swine, or whatever else you may choose to call them, has resulted in demand exceeding supply. This means they are expensive pets, and in turn this means that there are already those who are trying to cash in on them. A pot-belly will cost you anything from $300 upwards. Fees of over $30,000 are reputed to have been paid for high-quality minia-

With pot-bellies being in such great demand, there are, unfortunately, people who will crossbreed them with non-mini pigs—or use other unscrupulous methods—to cash in on the pot-bellied pig craze.

ture sows. For this kind of money, there are those that will forge pedigrees and cross-breed pot-bellies to other pigs in order to try and obtain some quick cash. Here could be a classic case of "buy in haste and repent at leisure."

In this book it is hoped that you will find all of the information you need in order to decide if the pot-belly is for you and your family. You will not only read about how to go about purchasing one or more of these fascinating pets but also how to feed it and care for it. While the pig as a farm animal is known to everyone, the average person knows little or nothing about its place in the world of animals. For this reason, the natural history of the pig is included for the first time in a book devoted to these pets.

No single volume on a pet-animal subject can ever be truly definitive because new information periodically comes to light. This stated, you will find that all of what is currently known about these miniature pigs has been included within the following chapters. You will have at your fingertips a concise yet complete work that in its text and photographs provides you with the ideal source of reference for the pot-bellied pig.

Suidae—The Pig Family

In this chapter you can read about the place that the pig holds in the world of animals. It is not a subject that is essential to your ability to choose and care for a pot-bellied pig, but most pet owners like to know something about the life of the wild cousins of their pets. This can sometimes be helpful in understanding what their pets' needs are and is certainly a very interesting subject.

In order that any animal can be referred to without confusion, and in such a way that its features, and those of all other creatures, are placed in some sort of logical form, a system of classification was devised during the 18th century by a Swedish naturalist named Carolus Linnaeus. It has been modified over the years, but the basis of it remains as applicable today as it was when it was first conceived.

The system is known as the binomial system of classification. It uses a mixture of Latin, Greek, and other languages in order to name, or identify, every living animal and plant. The system and the nomenclature used are totally international in acceptance—surely one of the very few things on which people from every single nation have come to agree.

THE WAY CLASSIFICATION WORKS

All living organisms are grouped into one of two kingdoms: plant and animal. The latter is formally known as Animalia. Based on shared features, the animals are divided into many hundreds of groups in a manner that is thought to represent their phylogenic (evolutionary) relationship. If you will imagine a triangle, then the apex is the kingdom Animalia, while the baseline is composed of all the many thousands of differing life forms that we call species.

Opposite: Loins, hocks, or chops...No matter how you slice it, the pig has primarily been kept as a source of food. Today however, the pot-belly can proudly point to a loftier role in the animal kingdom: that of family pet.

Pot-bellied pigs can have litters that range anywhere from one to twelve, but four to eight is more typical. Female pot-bellies, in general, are very good mothers.

THE CLASS

At each level within this system, group names, which represent given features, are used. All the members in a given group (or taxon) possess all or many of the features associated with the group. As you progress down from the all-embracing kingdom, the animals in the groups are progressively more closely related to each other than to those in other groups. For example, one group is called a class, and all the members of a given class have similar features. All birds are found in the class Aves, while all snakes and lizards are in the class Reptilia. The bony fish are found in the class Osteichthyes, and all the animals that suckle their young, have hair, and reproduce using a placenta, are in the class called Mammalia— the mammals.

We humans are mammals, as are tigers, dogs, cows, elephants, whales and some 4,500 other species—including the pig as well. A pig, a human, and a tiger are clearly very different from each other, yet obviously have more in common with each other than they do to a reptile or a bird.

THE ORDER ARTIODACTYLA

The group or rank of class is divided into further groups known as orders. Again, within each order all of the members will have similar features. Two very well-known orders are those of Carnivora and Primates. The former contains all the flesh-eaters: cats, dogs, bears and many others. The latter houses the great apes, all the monkeys, and, of course, us humans. Once again, you will see that within the order the animals are more closely related to each other than to those of other orders.

Pigs are grouped in the order called Artiodactyla, the even-toed ungulates. An ungulate is an animal that has hooves. The hoof is equivalent to a human's nail but, of course, is very much larger and stronger. Animals that walk on their nails are said to be unguligrade, as opposed to those that walk on the soles of their feet (plantigrade), or on their toes (digitigrade). The closest relatives to pigs are hippopotamuses, camels, llamas, deer, giraffes, and bovids (antelope, cattle, goats and sheep).

Horses, zebras, tapirs, and rhinoceroses are also unguligrade, but they are grouped within the order Perissodactyla, the odd-toed ungulates. They are not quite so closely related to pigs as are the others mentioned.

A pig has four toes on each foot, two of the toes being small and placed on either side of the larger medial ones. The latter are termed cloven because they are visibly divided.

There are some 211 species of artiodactyls, many of which are ruminants. This means they possess a four-chambered stomach that allows them to regurgitate their food. Cows, for example, are said to "chew the cud." Pigs have a simple two-chambered stomach, and so they are not ruminants.

THE FAMILIES SUIDAE AND TAYASSUIDAE

The order Artiodactyla is divided into nine families, two of which are of particular interest to the pig enthusiast. They are Suidae, the pigs, and Tayassuidae, the peccaries. In total, the two families comprise only 12 species, nine of these being in Suidae. This makes the pig and peccary families very small when compared to most other mammalian families.

Although pigs and peccaries are superficially very similar, more so than pigs and wart hogs, which are actually more closely related, it is in not-so-obvious features that they differ from each other. The pig (with one exception) has six pairs of teats, whereas peccaries have either two or four pairs. The digestive system of a peccary, while non-

Foaming at the mouth.
Boars generally tend to
do this more than sows.

There are a number of different varieties of miniature pig. The one that people are most familiar with is the Vietnamese pot-bellied pig.

ruminating, is somewhat more complex than that of a pig. A pig has a total of 44 teeth, while a peccary has only 38.

Further, the tusks (elongated canine teeth) of the peccary point downward, while in pigs they grow out and upward, and are also larger in size. There are also differences in the toe formation in peccaries, as well as in other features which, collectively, make them different enough to justify placing them in their own family. However, in their general way of life, pigs and peccaries are both very similar. Each lives in groups and forages in the undergrowth for food. Both pigs and peccaries are renowned for their great valor when facing an adversary. Apart from their great weight and solid muscle, pigs and peccaries are armed with potentially lethal razor-sharp tusks.

Peccaries in particular confront their would-be predators as a group. As such, they can prove more than a match for even the largest of jaguars, coyotes, or mountain lions. Many a hunter has found he is really not so brave, even with a gun, when hunting peccaries in scrub country. If one member of a family is shot, the rest will often charge and tree the hunter! Pigs are also stalwart fighters that combine speed of foot with a tenacity and ferocity that has left many a predator wishing it had never tried to have pork chops for dinner!

THE GENUS

The family is divided into a number of genera (singular: genus). In Suidae, there are five, that of *Sus* being the largest. The other four each contain but a single species. At generic level the close affinity of the members is becoming very clear, yet we can still perceive obvious differences. Thus, a genus is divided into a number of species.

THE SPECIES

A species is a group of similar animals that will

Opposite: The successful domestication of the pig lies in the fact that it did not directly compete with other farm livestock and was content to scavenge leftovers.

freely interbreed under natural conditions. In formal classification this is the lowest rank or group, but you may no doubt be aware that there are also subspecies. These are interbreeding groups that show minor anatomical differences from others that are clearly of the same species. Usually, subspecies are separated by some geographic barrier, such as a mountain range or a wide river.

The binomial system of nomenclature gives every living organism (animal or plant) its own unique name. By so doing, no two creatures can ever be confused, which is often the case when common names, such as African, or Asian, pig, are used. The scientific name for a given animal is made up of two parts. The first is the name of the genus; the second is the specific name within that genus. While a specific (or trivial) name may be used for differing animals, it can never be used twice in the same

genus. Thus, when the genus and specific names are placed together, they form a unique name.

The genus *Sus* contains five species. Each displays its own form and differs from the others in the genus. Our interest lies with the species known as *Sus scrofa,* which is more commonly referred to as the wild boar or pig. It is also called a swine or a hog, but as each of these names can be equally applied to all the members of the family Suidae, the importance of the scientific name becomes apparent. It designates one particular type of pig or hog: *Sus scrofa*, the wild pig.

In scientific parlance, generic or species names always appear in a type that differs from that of the main text. Thus, they are normally seen in italics. Note also that the genus always commences with a capital letter, while the trivial name always commences with a lowercase letter.

The wild pig *S.scrofa*

Pot-bellied pigs enjoy the same status as that of a more traditional family pet: the dog. (Pot-bellies can get along well with dogs if they are introduced early on and properly supervised.)

enjoys an extensive range of distribution that stretches from mainland Europe, through northern Africa, to Asia as far as Siberia and Japan. It was formerly also native to Britain but was hunted out of existence. Its northern distribution is thought to have been restricted by snow, in which it is seasonally found but in which it is not suited to live in on a permanent basis. Like all other members of its family, it is thus a creature of the Old World, whereas peccaries are its equivalent in the New World.

In the wild, this species may attain a weight of up to 770 lbs. (350kg), which is an awful lot of bacon to come at you if it charges! Shoulder height may reach 110cm (43 in.), so a wild boar is quite a lot taller than a Saint Bernard dog and about three times heavier. However, this is an optimum size, and it is doubtful if any wild pigs of this size are left on earth—most are much smaller today. In contrast, some domestic forms may exceed the weight quoted by as much as 220 lbs. (100kg).

In color, wild pigs appear black, gray or brown, though the hair is actually of the agouti type (banded in black, brown, and yellow) to a greater or lesser degree. The hair is sparse but substantially more dense than in most domestic forms. Its texture is wiry. The tail is straight, never curled as in domestic pigs. The ears are large and erect, though not as large as in some domestic forms. One very important difference between true wild pigs and the domestic forms is that the piglets of the former are striped. This feature has been lost in farmyard varieties.

Although the female can theoretically breed at any time of the year, this is often related to the seasons, usually following the rains— when food will be more plentiful. A sow will generally only have one litter per year, and the young will be weaned after about four months. A male will not normally mate a sow until he is about 4 to 5 years of age. This is because he is not physically fully mature until then, thus unable to compete with the established boars for a harem.

The family unit is invariably made up of a sow with her offspring of varying ages, the mature males leading a solitary life. During the breeding period, the sow will leave her family unit and be part of the male's harem, which will range in number from 1 to 9. Once the young are born, the females will come together with their babies and will later rejoin their offspring of earlier matings. A herd will usually comprise about 12 to 20 individuals, but it can reach 100 in regions that will sustain such numbers (and which are free of human hunters).

In respect of their diet, wild pigs are omnivorous, meaning they eat foods of both vegetable and animal origin. The main diet is made up of wild vegetables, fungi, plant roots, grasses, cereals, fallen nuts, indeed almost anything that grows. They will also eat insects and other invertebrates, small snakes, eggs, and any carrion that comes their way. In short, they can truly be said to be pigs! However, contrary to popular belief, wild pigs are not unduly gluttonous. They are heavy animals so need to maintain their weight. But they are also extremely nimble of foot, so will carry no more fat than is appropriate to their size.

Their famed love for mud baths is, however, quite true. This is because they have few sweat glands, so they cool the body by wallowing in muddy water whenever the opportunity arises. This also helps to moisten their otherwise hard, dry skin.

The species *Sus scrofa* has been introduced to just about every country in the world where it was non-native—thus Australia, New Zealand,

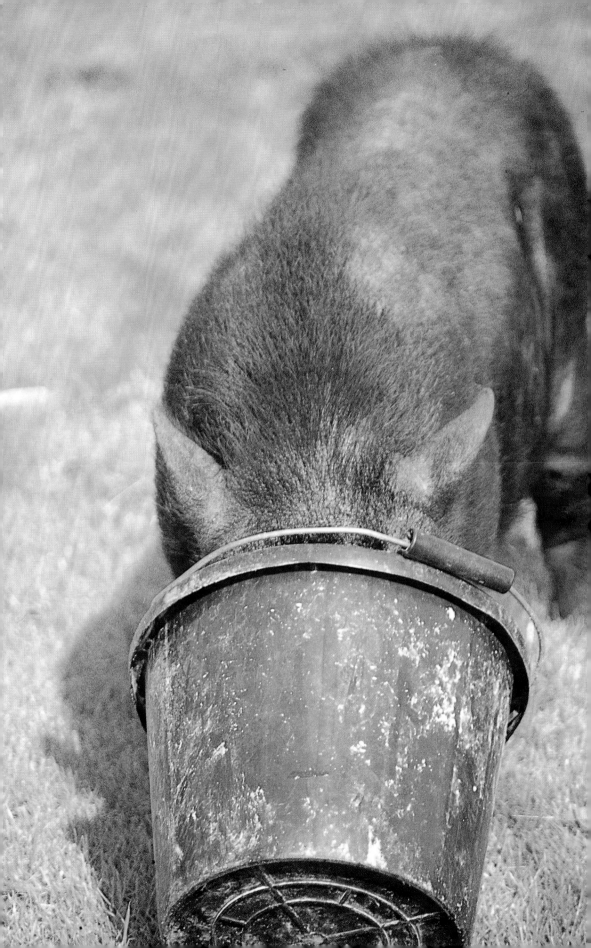

Pigs live to eat and will eat just about everything. They are easily capable of becoming obese, which is not desirable for your pot-bellied pet.

North America, and many islands. As a result of domestic pigs' escaping, there are many feral pigs to be found around the world. In some instances, they have proved very destructive to the indigenous flora and fauna. This has also resulted in a situation where it is not always possible to tell if the wild pigs are truly that, or if they are essentially feral pigs that have steadily reverted back to their natural form.

While *S.scrofa* is not endangered, the same cannot be said for other wild pigs. *Sus salvanius*, the pygmy hog of northern India, is on Appendix 1 of the CITES (Convention on International Trade in Endangered Species) list, while two other species, *S. barbatus* and *S.verrucosus*, must be regarded as at least vulnerable, due to habitat destruction and hunting in their native Asian lands. While the average person might not consider wild pigs the most pressing concern for the need of protection, the hard reality is that this is the case because they are so few in species numbers. They are as vital a part of our world as are any other creatures, great or small. It is hoped that the growing popularity of the pot-bellied pig may bring more awareness to the needs of this fascinating family of mammals.

THE WILD PIG BECOMES DOMESTIC

Whenever any person attempts to determine the domestication of a species within a time frame they immediately run into a major problem. This is the fact that for many animals the event happened prior to recorded history. This is certainly true of the pig, as it is with the dog, the sheep, the goat, the cow, and the chicken, which are almost certainly the first animals that humans domesticated. Apart from the matter of the time frame, there is also the question of where domestication commenced. The best we can do is to draw

Pot-bellied pigs can make wonderful family pets.

conclusions based on what we know of the earliest humans, and what we know of the lifestyles of the various animals that we have domesticated.

In the modern world, we do not need a specific practical reason to bring animals into our homes, but for our ancestors of the earliest times this was a fundamental prerequisite. There had to be a need to go out and capture wild creatures. This was, in most instances, prompted by a gastronomic urge. If an edible species could be caught and retained within an encampment, it could provide food for a later date. Once this matter had been accomplished, the next stage would be to try and breed the captive animals, as this would reduce the need to go out and hunt. It would also mean that the community could control the supply of food.

Another aspect of animal domestication revolved around the concept that this would only be possible if settlements were more or less permanent, or if the animal species was one that would not be difficult to herd and move from one grazing place to the next. Dogs, sheep, and goats are easy animals to move around, but the same is not true of pigs, which tend to live in small family units that wander within a fixed territory. Further, they tend to stay within regions that are never unduly short of water or vegetation on which they can feed. Putting these various aspects together, it is not unreasonable to suppose that the pig was first domesticated either in the more temperate regions of Europe, or the warmer climates of Asia—those that are also well forested, thus not short of water or vegetation. Certainly, most pig species are native to the more tropical countries of the latter land mass and its islands. In such lands, there was not the necessity to traverse vast distances in order to feed flocks of animals.

As holds true for many other kinds of animals, it is not known precisely when domestication of the pig occurred: estimates range from as early as 10,000 B.C. to as late as 2000 B.C.

Having established the likely regions of the pig's domestication, it is then a case of considering a time factor. Without written records, this becomes rather a calculated guessing business, of which no one can be sure. Normally, experts will look at the earliest cultures to provide clues, but this can be wildly inaccurate. With the information gained from more extensive excavations and the use of more sophisticated dating technology, archaeologists can place events and cultures further back in time. Presently, it is thought that pigs were first domesticated about 4900 B.C. but that it *may* have commenced as early as 10,000 B.C.— quite a difference. China and Thailand (formerly Siam) are cited as two likely places, due to the cultures that were being established in these countries. However, we should not assume domestication commenced at one point on the globe and then spread. It may well have happened concurrently in two or more regions where the needs of people, and the environment, may have been much the same. This is especially true in the case of *Sus scrofa*, whose natural range of distribution is extensive.

I have read that the first written record of pig rearing dated back to 3468 B.C. in China. However, I have also read that the legendary emperor Fu Hsi did not introduce writing in the form of hieroglyphics until about 2852 B.C. Other historians place the earliest crude writing to only 2000 B.C. You can therefore see the obvious problems in trying to trace domestication, even to periods when civilizations had become established.

Be this as it may, it would not be unreasonable to suppose that the Chinese may well have been one of the first peoples to actually develop recognized breeds or varieties. They were known to have developed a number of mouse and goldfish varieties by 1000 B.C., so we can be sure they would also have turned their talents to the development of farm stock.

THE MAKING OF PETS

Once pigs had become part of the everyday life of human communities, their virtuous qualities were no doubt quickly appreciated—as they have been ever since. They are extremely intelligent animals that display a considerable capacity to memorize things, and it is memory that makes for great intelligence. It is directly as a result of their mental prowess that they became popular pets.

They could be trained, and this is a very big plus for any animal that takes up residence with us humans. Pigs are also very affectionate and will quickly relate to those who reciprocate. The fact that they are also easy to feed, and reproduce rapidly under controlled conditions, gave the pig many appreciated qualities to those who first domesticated it.

As the centuries rolled by, many domesticated varieties were created in eastern countries. This situation persists to this day. In Europe too, stock breeders, by selective breeding, have recombined the most favorable pig genes to create a multitude of breeds, a number of which are much heavier than their original wild ancestors.

In eastern countries, as well as in Latin American nations, pigs in the more underdeveloped communities are allowed to run free around villages. They are invariably allowed into homes, where they will quickly devour any scraps of food found on the floor. They thus provide a sort of garbage disposal system, which is another of their virtues to those owning them. In some of the more remote villages of Tibet, pigs are also used in a home-guarding role. Like geese, they will attack any strangers who attempt to enter their domain at night. Their size and weight make them a creature not to be trifled with.

Throughout the ages, the pig has been variously maligned as dirty, gluttonous, and ill mannered. Dedicated pot-belly owners, who happily share their homes with these animals, will tell you that this simply isn't so.

Pigs have also been trained as trackers, for they have a very keen sense of smell—even if their eyesight might leave something to be desired. The full potential of pigs has never actually been thoroughly investigated simply because in the minds of most people they are farm animals bred to be eaten.

PIG MYTHS AND SAYINGS

A good indication of the way in which a given animal is regarded by humans can be gauged by the sayings that are associated with it. Unfortunately, history has hardly been kind to the pig. More than any other animal, it is regarded as being unclean and less than desirable. "Beware of buying a pig in a poke," for example, means you should take care lest you purchase an item that proves to be less than the genuine article, or is unreliable. "You can't make a silk purse out of a sow's ear" tells you that you cannot produce quality, or something desirable, from inferior material.

The inference is obviously that a pig is a lowly or inferior form of life. "He or she has the manners of a pig" clearly suggests that a pig is in someway short on etiquette! The same is true of "He or she eats like a pig," which suggests that the person is gluttonous and ill-mannered. "The house is like a pigsty" is yet another reference to the conceived notion that pigs are filthy creatures that have no notion of personal cleanliness. While most sayings about pigs revolve around the fact that they are ill-mannered and unclean, there are a few that suggest they are not too bright either. "What can you expect of a pig other than a grunt?" The saying that you should not try teaching a pig to sing because it will annoy the pig and waste your time is clearly based around the fact that the pig is not held to be capable of learning too much—and in any case has limited vocal potential, even if it could learn. "Pigs might fly" is used to relate to an impossibility. To say a person squeals like a pig suggests that the person lacks bravery, or has a rather low threshold of pain and will yell loudly at the slightest incidence of it. To say someone looks like a pig is to suggest they are ugly—and on and on we could go. One of the few sayings that has a double edge to it is that made by the famous British statesman Winston Churchill. He suggested that dogs look up to us and cats look down on us (he was a avid cat lover), while pigs treat us as equals!

The irony of all of these sayings is that they reflect on the pig based on the way humans have treated pigs, rather than on the actual qualities of the animal. In other words, we have created the filth and unclean conditions that we force the pig to live in! If pigs eat garbage around our homes, it is because we have placed the garbage there in the first place. If we cannot provide suitable living conditions—given the size and weight of a pig—then it is hardly the pig's fault if it smells and has an untidy home. It merely indicates how poorly we have attended to routine cleaning chores.

A large pig (and pot-bellies are never that) can be a very dangerous animal if it is mistreated—but so will any other creature. Reared with kindness, a pig is totally trustworthy and predictable. However, you must understand its basic character and the times when it is less reliable. This is equally true of elephants, rhinos, large parrots, and many other animals that may display less than their usual behavior during breeding periods. It is indeed unfortunate that humans choose to attach sayings, and thus imply characteristics, to animals, because they become implanted in our minds. They invariably totally distort the truth of the creature so maligned.

Since their
arrival in the
USA in 1985,
miniature pot-
bellied pigs
have enjoyed
ever-growing
popularity as
pets.

THE POT-BELLY BECOMES A PET

While the pot-bellied pig has been in existence for many centuries in eastern countries, it is only since about 1985 that its virtues as a pet were appreciated in the western world. Prior to 1985, the only place where you would see a pot-bellied pig would have been within a zoological park, where they are labeled as Vietnamese. The zoo pot-belly is rather different from the pet version in one important area: size. The ideal pet is a miniature version of the variety, though many pets are actually larger and heavier than the ideals that pot-belly associations are striving to establish as a standard.

The foundation stock of these pets in the USA was imported in 1985 from Europe into Canada by Keith Connell, a zoo director. From the offspring resulting from matings of the original imports many present day pot-bellies are derived. A second major importation of pot-bellies to North America was made in 1989 by Keith Leavitt of Texas. The Connell and Lea lines are thus the two most well-known lines to which most American pot-bellies can be traced. Once the first few pigs began to find new homes in the USA, a number of people took up breeding them and have already become very well established in the hobby.

Many exotic pets come and go almost unnoticed, so it is a matter of chance whether or not a "new" pet can establish itself. As it happened, the pot-belly gained some excellent promotion via the TV and glossy periodicals and has not looked back since. To a lesser extent, the same is happening with the llama and its relatives (which are also artiodactyls).

The rise of the pot-belly has not been without a beneficial overflow to other existing miniature pigs. They have been bred in the

Pigs can be taught to use a litterbox. For purposes of hygiene, regularly change the litter and disinfect the litterbox.

USA and Europe for over two decades (and more recently also in Australia), principally by research laboratories, where the virtues of miniature pigs are self evident. Some of the recognized varieties are the Yucatan miniature, which is hairless, the Hormel, the Pitman-Moore, the Juliana, the African Guinea, and the Swedish white, to name but a few. The care of any of the other miniature pigs is no different to that of the pot-belly, so if you are also thinking of any other mini-pig varieties, this book will serve your needs.

I should point out that the term *miniature* is a relative term in many breeds. For example, if a farm pig can reach a weight of over 1,000 lbs., a specimen of the same variety that tips the scales at no more than 300 lbs. is a miniature. But that still makes it a hefty piece of pork if it was to be kept within your home. The pot-belly is altogether smaller and lighter.

At the present time, the target of breeding in the pot-belly is mainly centered around size, but already some breeders are turning their attention to color and pattern. Apart from the traditional black, the white and the pinto are well established. You can expect to see blues, grays, browns, reds, tans, and patterns involving these colors, to be developed in the coming years, even if some are not initially readily accepted within the pot-belly hobby.

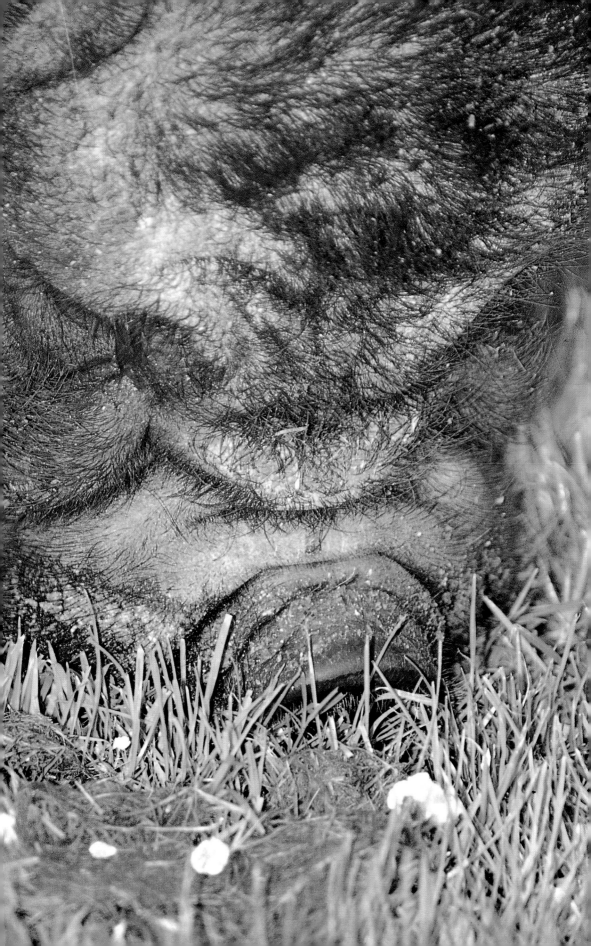

Despite its bulky size, a pot-bellied pig can move with a good amount of speed...especially when it comes to food.

Think Before You Buy

The first thing that should be established in this chapter is that it is by no means the objective of this book to sell you on the idea of owning a pot-bellied pig. Indeed, if you have any reservations about such an undertaking and what follows plants further doubts in your mind, it will have achieved a useful purpose. It would be better that you admire these pets but never own one. Conversely, if your mind is made up that you intend to purchase one, then the following will act as a reminder of the things you must be aware of, and of your responsibilities.

LEGAL ASPECTS

Before making a decision to own a pot-bellied pig, the first thing to be done is to find out if you will be able to do so in terms of complying with the regulations that may be in force in your area. They may be local, state, or federal, so you must look into this aspect. The best place to start is with your municipal clerk. He or she will probably be aware of any restrictions with regard to pigs. You will need to determine the status of the pot-belly (or, more especially, that of the pig, because in most areas the pot-belly is not classed as anything other than farm livestock). With the latter thought in mind, your problems will be less likely if you live in a rural farming location where you know other farm livestock are kept. Within city limits, there will be some form of ordinances that relate to the keeping of pets, be they domestic or exotic. An exotic is normally any animal that is non-native to your state, region, or country, and it may be that this will be how the pot-belly will be perceived. However, in most urban areas, pigs are designated as farm livestock and as such are generally not

Opposite: Obtaining a pot-bellied pig is a very exciting undertaking, so it behooves you to control your impatience and to avoid rushing into things. This will make the time that your piglet eventually arrives in your home one that you will cherish for years to come.

There are many aspects to consider before purchasing your pot-bellied pig. One of the most important is the status of the pig according to your municipality's legal codes. Be fully aware of any such laws before you bring home the bacon.

permitted. This is most certainly true when it comes to breeding them.

In the matter of breeding, federal restrictions may apply. The pot-belly will be viewed as farm livestock and thus under the control of the appropriate ministry of agriculture, farm and fisheries, or whatever department fulfills that role in your country. Also be aware that interstate transportation of a pig may also be a legality you may need to consider, both when purchasing a pot-belly and when vacationing (if you decide to take your pig along and the route crosses a state line). The fact is that the pot-belly is such a new pet that its status has not actually been defined. Now, you may be told by a seller that many people keep these pets and do not check out the legal status and have never been prosecuted or even contacted by official departments. Take no notice of such advice. If you gamble on this happening in your

instance, always bear in mind that it takes only one disapproving neighbor to make a complaint, and the appropriate authorities will be in touch. They can confiscate your pet and order it be slaughtered or otherwise disposed of. Do you wish to take this chance? Check out the full legal status before you buy, thus saving yourself a lot of heartache down the line.

THE INVESTMENT VALUE OF POT-BELLIES

It may be that you are interested in breeding pot-bellies as a lucrative investment. If this is so, be prepared to lose money big time! It is true that at the time of writing these pigs do represent an excellent return on investment. But how long will this situation pertain? Many breeders work on the assumption that zoning laws will be changed to embrace the pot-belly, thus the market will expand for some years. Do not count on this because I very much doubt laws will be changed unduly to meet the needs of pet owners—especially where farm livestock is concerned. It is probably more likely that local ordinances will be introduced to specifically outlaw pigs being kept as pets in urban situations. From a legal standpoint, if pot-bellies are allowed in urban areas, there becomes little grounds for denying the keeping of sheep, goats, or even cows, as pets, so petitioning for changes in the law may not prove especially productive. Further, it takes only one irresponsible pet owner to be identified as having broken a legal requirement with regard to disease protection. Thus, all pet owners might suffer.

Also, you should be mindful of the fact that breeding pigs are not good pets within a home environment, especially boars.

PIGS AND GARDENS

Pot-bellied pigs just love gardens. They will especially enjoy uprooting and eating just about everything you have planted, from roses to cucumbers! On a hot day the feel of some cool earth beneath them is most enticing, so a good roll in it will be their idea of soothing enjoyment. They will also root about on your lawn, though more often than not they will not damage it. Their main focus of interest will be in eating the weeds that grow in it, which may not actually displease you. If your garden is not totally fenced, then you had better make a pig pen. Otherwise, your pets will as happily munch away on your neighbors' prize flowers! Remember, pigs are intelligent. They will devise a way to escape their pen if it is possible, so build to a good standard.

PIGS INDOORS

Even a *small* pig in the home can be a riot squad, especially where food is concerned. Many are the stories of pigs raiding the refrigerator for a snack while their owners are asleep or at work. A snack to a healthy pot-belly will

While it is true that some apartment dwellers successfully keep mini pigs as pets, the best environment for a pig is one that provides him with ample opportunity for exercise and fresh air. Additionally, the animal must have an area in which it can root around.

mean just about everything in the fridge, and anything else that is edible in the kitchen as well. They will leave nothing unturned in an effort to appease their undoubted appreciation of all food items. Their intelligence again comes into play, and their muscular snout makes a super cupboard or refrigerator door opener. Everything must always be continually kept almost under lock and key. Additionally, a pig should not be given free run of the house if it is home alone.

Pigs are not the most delicate of pets when moving around a home. While a dog or cat will normally go around things, a pig is so powerful that it may, especially when excited or frightened, go straight through them, metaphorically speaking. Valuable ornaments, as well as potted indoor plants (many can be poisonous), should be kept well away from your pet pig.

Highly polished floors and pigs do not go well together. These pets do not have anything like the grip on smooth surfaces that cats and dogs do, so do not overlook this aspect. When they decide to sit or lie on a chair, be aware that the pressure placed on their little trotters (hooves) is considerable—this then being transferred to your furniture. Unless it is very solid, the fabric may not last too long.

APARTMENT PIGS

You may read that pigs are ideal apartment pets. This is misguided advice that looks impressive in glossy magazines. It is true that a pot-belly does have a number of features that would make it an excellent pet for an apartment, but there are other considerations that are the opposite. The most important of them (apart from zoning restrictions) is the fact that pigs need to be given plenty of exercise if they are to remain fit. They do not ascend or descend stairs well. They should also have access to earth in which to root around. If

Reared with kindness,
a pig is totally
trustworthy.

these natural needs are not met, the owner stands accused of pandering only to his own desires—with no consideration of the needs of the pet. A pet's needs should be paramount to any pet lover.

THE ADULT PET PIG

Many people purchase pets because when the animals are babies, they are cute, cuddly, saucy, and great fun to have around the home. They grow up very quickly. A puppy or a kitten will remain very active for most of its life. Not so the pot-belly, which will slow down considerably once mature. Its skin will be dry and hard to the touch. Its longevity has not actually been established at this time, but it may well live to around 20 years of age. Will you be as keen to keep it during the last 19 years as you were in the first? Will it become an inconvenience to you come vacation time? Consider how many unwanted pets you know of that roam the streets, or are taken to

animal shelters. They are testimony of just how many people think they are pet lovers but really aren't. If you do not honor your commitment, be assured you will not be popular in your locality if your pet pig is roaming loose. Nor should it be condemned to a pen in your yard once it reaches maturity. Neglected and lacking the affection shown to it as a youngster, it will become another sad case of an uncared for pet.

THE VIRTUES OF THE POT-BELLIED PIG

Having discussed the down side of owning a pig, let us now consider its virtues as a pet and in so doing bury some of the myths that have built up around it for centuries. Being an intelligent animal, it is easy to train any pig breed, and the pot-belly is no different. It is a very social pet and so will greatly enjoy your company and develop a strong bond with you and your family—if it is reared with kindness. It

A family of pot-bellies and their canine companion exploring the grounds. Pigs are livestock, and, as such, can be subject to additional legal restrictions, e.g., when it comes to breeding.

will get along very well with any other pets in your household, such as dogs and cats. It will also get along very well with other pigs, especially if they are reared together from a young age. If not, a period of sorting out their hierarchal positions will be necessary. Pigs are friendly with other farm livestock, including sheep, goats, cattle, and horses.

They can be trained to a lead, so they can be taken for a walk—just like a dog. As they are not very fast-moving pets (once they have matured), you will not have the problem of them taking you for a walk! The pot-belly is not an expensive pet to care for in terms of its diet. It will, of course, eat just about anything, which is why most rural Chinese families own pigs. Nothing is wasted with a pig around the house.

While an untrained dog that continually barks can really offend a neighbor, as can a raucous parrot, this will not be so with your piggy. Pigs are quiet animals, and normally the only time you will hear any noise, other than a muted grunt, is if they are frightened or hurt, at which time they will emit a high-pitched squeal.

Pigs are very clean creatures and can be house trained to use a litter tray, as well as a dog door, to attend to their toiletry needs. Of course, if you do not pay prompt attention to cleaning their tray after each use, there will be an odor. However, this applies equally to a cat, a dog, or any other mammal kept in a home.

The hair of a pig is sparse and coarse, relative to that of a dog or cat. This can be a decided advantage to those who may be affected by animal hair. Further, pigs are not continually shedding hair as dogs and cats do. The hair that is shed will not be the same sort of problem on carpets and furniture as it is with the "big two" pets mentioned. Neutered or spayed pigs (according

Opposite: A pot-belly has many of the same basic requirements as those of other kinds of pets. It needs daily attention and care in order to thrive.

to sex) have virtually no smell if they are cared for correctly and live in a clean environment. This said, every animal releases body odors that may be detected by those not owning that particular pet, or who are not pet owners. The extent of hygiene maintained will determine the extent of odors.

For all the virtues of a pot-bellied pig, or any other animal, in the final analysis it always comes down to whether or not you find that particular pet pleasing. Also, are you prepared to cater to its needs for every single day that it lives with you? These are the two most important factors in pet ownership.

Those who purchase any animal because of its novel or exotic value make poor owners. Those who buy a pet because they think it can make them some quick and easy money are foolish. It is a case of really searching your mind and heart and asking yourself if you are prepared to commit to whatever it takes in order to share your home with a pot-bellied pig. You must be prepared to take the bad with the good because pigs, like all other animals, are living breathing creatures with feelings. They are not angels, ornaments, or materialistic things that should be purchased simply because the idea appeals at a given moment.

The world is full of unwanted and poorly-cared-for dogs, cats, rabbits, and many other pets, so there is no need to add pet pigs to this list. Owning a pot-bellied pig is a two-way arrangement, so think before you buy.

Purchasing a Pot-Bellied Pig

If you have purchased this book before going out and buying a pot-bellied pig, then you have already approached the matter with a very sound common-sense attitude. You might be surprised at just how many people purchase a pet they know nothing about, other than what the seller has told them, and then look for a book when they realize the seller did not really tell them much at all about the pet.

LOOK BEFORE YOU LEAP

Once you have decided to buy a pot-belly, your next objective should be to see as many as you can. This serves a number of purposes. You will get a better idea of what a typical specimen should look like in terms of size, appearance, color, and health. Equally as important, you will be able to discuss pigs with the sellers and make mental notes on how they treat and generally care for them. You will soon come to recognize those trying to make a fast buck on the back of a pet that has become popular.

A well-intentioned person will have no reservations about drawing your attention to the down side of these pets—just as this book has done. While they want to sell their piglets, this does not mean they wish to do so without consideration for both the pig and for the new owner. You should gather as much information as you can about these pets.

The pet shop is, naturally, an excellent source to investigate when purchasing your little pig. Depending on where you live, however, this might not be possible. If your pet shop doesn't stock these mini pigs, perhaps the dealer can order one for you. If all else fails, you can write to the pot-

Hogs and kisses...Yes, pigs
can be affectionate!

bellied pig associations for addresses of breeders in your area. Do not purchase by mail-order. While some breeders are totally reliable, others are less so. In any case, if you are genuinely concerned about obtaining the right pig, you should be prepared to travel in order to personally select your pet and see the conditions under which it has been reared. Failure to do this is taking an unnecessary risk; and given the price of these pets, would seem a very foolish way to go about things.

However, the reality is that in countries such as the USA, the distance to the nearest breeder may be considerable. If you do decide to order without first seeing your prospective pet, then do so only from those breeders whose reputations are beyond doubt and who have been highly recommended to you. Make your decision carefully.

OTHER MINIATURE PIGS

As a full-time professional writer on all kinds of pets, I often encounter a recurring situation that I will tell you about because it may be applicable to you. Many people decide to purchase a given pet—be it a parrot, a dog, a cat or a rabbit—based on the appearance of someone else's pet. They may not be aware of just how many alternatives there really are to the breed they have decided to obtain. Later, they come to see these other varieties and will state that had they known about them, this would have affected their selection decision.

The pot-bellied pig has been projected into the limelight, but it is by no means the only miniature pig. If it is the notion of owning a pig, rather than specifically a pot-belly, that appeals to you, then in fairness to yourself you should make enquiries about the numerous other varieties and try to see them—or at least pictures of them. It may be that one of them may appeal more, or it may confirm your desire to own a pot-belly. Some have been established for a longer period of

According to the standard, the maximum allowable weight for a pot-bellied pig is 95 lbs; the ideal weight is about 50 lbs. However, depending on their breeding and feeding, some may grow to well over 150 lbs.

time and are more predictable in terms of height and weight. Others are available in a greater range of colors and patterns. In all instances, the advice in this chapter is applicable.

BUYER BEWARE

It is not difficult to sell people a "pig in a poke" if they clearly show they know nothing at all about pot-bellied pigs. As there is good money being earned selling these pets, it is no surprise that there are those that would sell you any(!) pig if you were gullible enough to hand over your money. Some will claim their pigs are pot-bellied when they are, in fact, crossbreeds. Others will try to sell you other miniature pig breeds at pot-bellied prices, or at greatly reduced prices.

It is not unknown for a person to have purchased a regular pig thinking he had bought a pot-belly. Once it started to mature into a "giant," the buyer quickly learned the error of his foolish ways. All

pot-bellies should carry a registration certificate that indicates their line of descent. A short pedigree will also be available. Check out the registration with the association that issued it.

Remember though, a piece of paper is only as good as the pig that bears it, this applying to both registrations and pedigrees. You must know from the outset what a pot-bellied piglet looks like. The photos in this book will show you, and your other research will likewise have established this.

Obviously, breeders recommended by associations should be trustworthy, but there are "black sheep" in all hobby pursuits who may well keep and breed a given pet.

THE MATTER OF SIZE AND WEIGHT

If the ultimate mature size and weight of your pot-bellied pig is of paramount importance to you, then maybe you should reconsider ownership. You must understand that at this stage of the development of the pet pot-belly, not all piglets may retain the small size and weight about which you have been told.

Breeding for size alone, with no consideration to health and vigor, is probably the singular biggest error committed by breeders in many pet hobbies. This becomes even more so when breeders are working with limited gene pools in which negative effects of small size have not had time to be fully investigated. The degree of inbreeding in pot-bellies is, of necessity, much higher as an overall population than in most other pets you could name. This is due to the restricted initial number of breeding lines.

This means that your major consideration should be with respect to health, not just to size and weight. The recognized standard for pot-bellied pigs cites ultimate objectives rather than present realities, so bear this in mind. The standard requires that these pigs should be no more than 18 in. (46cm) at the shoulder and that 14 in. (36cm) is more desirable. Some specimens will be larger than the heights given and could reach 20 in. (51cm). The weight is a maximum of 95 lbs. (43kg), and the target weight is about 50 lbs. (22.7kg). Present-day pot-bellies may tip the scales at any weight up to, or even beyond, 150 lbs. (68kg), depending on their breeding and feeding.

The standard is based on pigs of one year of age, but these pets are not fully mature at this time. The female will reach physical maturity when about 18-24 months, whereas the male may take until it is 3-5 years old before it attains its ultimate mature size and weight.

Seeing the parents will give you some idea of the likely size of the piglets, but this is by no means a certainty when viewing small pot-bellied parents. Only time can establish lines that are consistently small,

Pot-bellied pig fanciers differ in their preference as to which sex makes the better pet. No matter which sex you choose, it is important that your pet be neutered (males) or spayed (females).

because a number of generations must be selectively bred from to make the genes in the line more homozygous (purebreeding) for this trait. It is therefore prudent to adopt a flexible approach to ultimate size so that you are not disappointed should this exceed your expectations.

WHICH SEX?

As a general comment, I personally feel that the female is the better choice for the average pet owner, especially if the pig is to be kept in your home. This recommendation is not based on the fact that the female is more affectionate, but that from a purely practical viewpoint, females of virtually all mammalian species have less body odors than do males. Contrary to the situation that pertains to farmyard pigs, the female pot-belly invariably grows to a larger size than the male. However, there are so many variables in respect of size that for all practical purposes,

the size of the sexes can be discounted as a factor that should influence choice.

Regardless of the sex, a pet pig *must* be neutered or spayed (the former for the male, the latter for the female). If this is not attended to, you will experience problems down the line. The unneutered male, a boar, will release a strong odor via its urine and its breath. It will tend to be more dominant in its mannerisms, thus more likely to be aggressive on occasion. He will go through regular periods of wanting to find a sow, so will be much more strenuous in his efforts to find a way out of his home. The barrow, a neutered male, is far more placid, will not smell as much, and generally will be more suited to the home environment.

The unspayed female will continually be coming into season over the course of a year, and she is much more moody and thus unpredictable during periods of her heat. At

Opposite:
Pot-bellied
pigs can be
black, pinto,
or white.
Through
selective
breeding, it is
possible that
other color
varieties will
be developed
in the future.

such times her only real interest is in finding a good boar! (If you have ever owned a female cat that has not been spayed, you will know exactly what I mean.)

COLOR

The basic color of this breed is black, but both pinto (black and white) as well as whites are available. The whites are not albinos, which is clear from the fact they generally have blue eyes, rather than unpigmented pink ones. White in pigs is transmitted as a recessive gene. The gene that creates white patches in pigs is also a recessive. This means it must be passed from each parent (a double dose) before it can be seen. Those pigs that display the belted pattern of white around the forequarters will probably be carrying the gene for this pattern, which is inherited as a dominant. (It is possible for a belted-type pattern to be the result of the white-spotting gene as well.)

There are well over 30 mutant genes (including at least 14 that are lethal) in pigs. A number of them will be found in the pot-belly. As other breeds are crossbred with pot-bellies in order to widen the color range, so more of the known genes will, of course, be established—for better or for worse—in the breed. If you have an interest in genetics, which is useful if you plan to become a breeder, you are advised to obtain any works relevant to the genetics of farm-pig breeds. If you already have a knowledge of genetics, then I should mention that the agouti pattern of the wild pig is not found in domestic pig breeds. The black coloration is, therefore, not non-agouti but is a result of the dominant extension gene E.

TAIL

The tail in this breed is straight—never curly. The curly tail is found in farmyard breeds and is the result of a recessive gene that is called kinky tail. If you see a kinked tail in pot-bellied piglets,

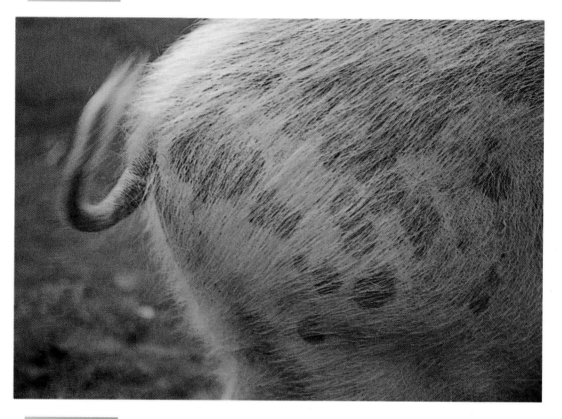

Pot-bellied pigs have straight tails. A pot-belly that evidences curliness in its tail has crossbreeding to a farmyard variety in its heritage.

this indicates that crosses to farmyard varieties have been made at some point in the breeding program. Although the pot-belly is a domesticated breed, it has always retained the wild-type tail. It is, of course, possible that an independent mutation for kinked tail could appear without having been transferred from another breed. The more numerous a breed becomes, the greater the chance of new mutations appearing independently in it.

When this happens, it creates the obvious problem of deciding if the mutation is derived from the breed or from crossings with other breeds. This situation often causes controversy in a breed. A result of this is that the various associations may or may not accept new colors or forms as being of that breed. If not, a new breed is thus created and is given a new name.

GENERAL FEATURES

The eye color of pot-bellies can be dark brown or blue. Eye color is certainly related to body color but not necessarily in any fixed and predictable manner. Other factors are involved, which means that as other body colors are developed eye color may become more variable.

A characteristic feature of the mature pot-bellied pig is that it has a pot belly, which hangs down and may even rub the floor. It also has a swayed back: a dip in the middle of the back as though the weight of its belly was pulling the back down. The ears are erect, but in poor specimens they may show some weakness or floppiness. Such a situation can also be the result of cross breeding, in which the incomplete dominance of the erect ear gene of farmyard breeds has been introduced by accident via crosses. The nose is short and snub, exhibiting variable degrees of wrinkling. It should not be long, which would again suggest either extremely poor quality, or more likely that the pig was a crossbreed.

The legs are short and straight. Again, variation in leg structure is the result of either poor breeding or crossing with poor-quality domestic pigs. When viewed in profile, the forehead of a pot-bellied pig should display a nice curve and should not be flat. Length of the body should be proportionate to the size of the animal. Only by viewing many pigs will this provide you with a mental idea of what good proportions should be like. The feet are small and compact. The hooves should be inspected to see if they are well shaped and in no way deformed.

It is unlikely you will be able to inspect the dentition of the piglet, but for the record the breed has 28 deciduous teeth and 44 permanent teeth.

VETERINARY CERTIFICATE

You are strongly recommended to insist that any piglet you purchase comes with a veterinary certificate of health, issued within 48 hours of your collecting the pet. Even with this, you are advised to take the pig to your own veterinarian in order to get a second opinion. This will be crucial in the event the piglet becomes ill within days of your obtaining it. Pot-bellies can suffer from all of the same diseases found in farm pigs, so appropriate vaccinations are essential.

AGE TO PURCHASE

Domestic pigs are normally weaned as they reach the age of about 4-5 weeks. However, it may be best to wait until the youngster is 7-8 weeks before you take it home. This ensures it should be feeding very well on its own. The first few weeks of any animal's life are very important, and this is doubly so where pigs are concerned. The mortality rate is high during the first few weeks, so you need to be very sure the baby is well established and very healthy before you acquire it. If you are purchasing from a reputable breeder, this will certainly be the case.

Pigging out. Don't lavish food on your pig as a means of showing that you care for him: obesity in pot-bellies can present serious health problems.

If you are away from home for long periods during the day, it would be better to purchase a piglet that is older, say 10-12 weeks of age. However, being very honest, if no one is in your home for most of the day, I would seriously question whether you should even have a pot-bellied pig as a pet. If you plan to become a breeder, there is merit in purchasing an established sow because you will be able to see her size and quality more readily. Of course, such a sow would be very much more expensive than a youngster. A quality boar or sow will command a substantial sum of cash.

THE PURCHASE PRICE

The old maxim of "You get what you pay for" is very true with these new pets. A pot-bellied piglet that is advertised at a remarkably low price is probably not a genuine pot-belly. If you see an adult pet mini-pig advertised at a low price, then you can just bet it is a delinquent pet and is best avoided. Always use caution when taking on an adult pet pig because there is usually some very sound (and often negative) reason why the owner wants to part with it. If the youngster has received all of its initial inoculations and has been neutered or spayed, it will, of course, cost more than the pet that has not been attended to.

You will appreciate that a breeder who has devoted much time to rearing a youngster in the confines of his home will charge more than a commercial breeder who simply breeds pot-bellied pigs as an investment.

Housing Pot-Bellied Pigs

There are two ways that you can choose from to accommodate your pet pig. One is in an outdoor pen, and the other is within your home. *Indoor housing is certainly the most preferable if you want to experience the joys of pig ownership at its best, and especially if you are planning to have only a single pig.* However, even in this instance, you are advised to also have some outdoor facility in which your porky friend can exercise and forage. He or she will greatly appreciate this on warm days.

If you plan to purchase a number of pot-bellies with a view to establishing a breeding line, that would be beyond the scope of this book. However, the comments made in respect of outdoor facilities would hold true, though would obviously need to be expanded to take account of the increased numbers.

LIVING IN THE HOME

If your new pet is to live within your home, most of its basic needs, such as protection from hot or inclement weather, will already be met. What you will need to do is to provide it with a comfortable place to sleep. You will also need to consider its penchant for constantly looking for culinary delights. The best way to overcome the problems that may arise from its inclination to seek out its own food would be to make the kitchen a "no-go for porky area," except when it is being fed under supervision. In open-plan kitchen arrangements, this may necessitate having a stylish half-door made to prevent the said porcine pet from entering the kitchen area unaccompanied. This may prove more convenient than having to fit pig-proof latches to all cupboard doors, as well as to the refrigerator. If you have what could be a slippery

Opposite: Have everything ready for your new piggy before he arrives in your home. This will make the period of acclimation a lot easier for both of you.

Opposite: Regular grooming is a must, especially if your pig spends a lot of time outdoors.

kitchen floor by a pig's standards, you might consider covering it with one of the hard-wearing kitchen carpets. This small concession will greatly reduce the risk of your pet slipping and maybe damaging a foot tendon.

With regard to the sleeping arrangements, they will either be in your bed, or in a specially made piggy bed. While some owners do allow their pets to sleep on their beds, what you should remember is that it is not fair to let this happen when the pet is a youngster and then forbid it as it gets older. Given its size and weight when mature, as well as its climbing limitations, it is suggested that your piggy friend should have its own bed from the outset. Pet shops stock large dog beds that are ideal for this purpose.

The main thing is that the bed must be very sturdy to take the pressure exerted by maybe 100 lbs. of bacon on four little hooves. Your pet should be able to lie stretched out when

sleeping: it is not a cat or a dog that will curl itself into a neat little ball. The bed should be low to the ground so the pig can get on and off it with ease. Pigs enjoy comfort, so the bed should be lined generously with blankets. Keep a number of them so that they can be washed on a regular basis, just as your own bedclothes are. Much of the time, your porcine pal will be quite happy just flopping down near you, or in a favored corner of the room.

OUTDOOR ACCOMMODATION

It is important that you try to erase from your memory the common concept of the typical farmyard pigsty. It is invariably too small and is not cleaned as it should be. The result is a dirty, smelly place—a veritable pigsty! Pigs are clean animals if given the opportunity to be so. They do not harbor fleas and other skin parasites as does the average dog or cat. This is because their skin is tough and

A well-designed piggery. It provides ample shelter and allows the occupants plenty of opportunity for fresh air and exercise.

Chow time. Keep your pig's mealtimes on a regular schedule. This will be better for his digestive system than if he were to be fed at varying hours each day.

their hair relatively sparse and coarse, giving pests nowhere to hide from sunlight and your watchful eyes.

The outdoor pig complex should comprise the shelter and the run. Ideally, the run will also open into a small paddock, in which porky can exercise and forage for food. Think in terms of an ideal dog kennel setup. The shelter can be made of wood or brick. Its height should be such that you can stand upright in it. If not, this will tend to hamper cleaning chores. The floor can be concrete for ease of cleaning, but it must have a generous covering of straw because pigs do not cope well on a slippery surface. In the shelter, you can place a large low wooden platform that has retaining walls on three sides. It can be filled with straw and will enable your pet to fashion a comfy warm nest in it.

The shelter should be light and airy. It must also be draftproof. Vents, both at the top and bottom of the walls, will enable you to create and regulate a comfortable circulation of air. There are no limits as to how fine a little home you can provide for your companion. Insulating the walls would certainly be worthwhile in most climates. You might even include some type of cooling unit, such as a ceiling fan, if you live in a hot region. Certainly, lighting is beneficial when it comes to attending to cleaning chores during the winter months—when it may be dark before you return home from work.

Heating is advisable in cold winter weather, whether you plan to breed or not. You can also provide a bed of woodshavings and dry leaves.

The shelter should stand on a concrete, or similar, base that provides an exterior-perimeter pathway. This will making cleaning easier. The roof of the shelter should have a generous overhang to help protect the walls. Be sure the roof is well

Opposite: A pig entering its shelter. The accommodation that you provide can be as plain or as fancy as you desire. Most importantly, it must provide shelter from the elements and should be large enough so that the animal can move around comfortably.

insulated and waterproofed. Guttering to carry rain water away is recommended in temperate regions. If you build the shelter using brick or other permanent materials, or if it is supplied with services such as water, sewerage and electricity, bear in mind that it may be subject to local zoning regulations—for which permissions and plans may be required. If you do plan to have two or more pot-bellied pigs, think in terms of incorporating a service and storage area in the shelter so that all needed cleaning items and food can be stored safely yet conveniently.

The run is simply an area where your pig can walk around and be contained yet enjoy some fresh air. Concrete is not the ideal surface, but it is a compromise that takes account of the need to maintain hygienic conditions within a restricted area. If soil is used, it will soon become contaminated with fecal matter and will become a mud hole after rain.

When laying the concrete, try to give it a *slight* rippled effect so it provides more grip for your pet's hooves. Be sure that the fencing to the run, and to the outer paddock, is erected to a good standard or your pet will escape, or stray dogs might enter to worry or attack the pig.

The run should incorporate some form of shade so your pet can escape the direct rays of the sun on very hot days. It should also feature a small wallowing pool (but one that will be large enough for the pig when it is fully mature). It should be shallow and easy to enter. All pigs enjoy bathing as it helps greatly in their keeping cool. They do not sweat, like some other animals, so can easily suffer if it is very hot. As a simple guide to temperature tolerance, you can assume that if you are outdoors and find it too cold, or too warm, so will your pot-bellied pig. In this and many other respects, pigs are actually very comparable to humans, as strange

Pigs are notoriously sloppy eaters. If you don't want your pig to dirty its house, feed it outdoors—weather permitting.

as it may seem.

In the wild, they sleep together for warmth. They will make a warm nest of leaves and other foliage under a suitable shrub. They will find cool spots under the forest canopy and will wallow in water or mud to cool and cleanse their skin. The paddock area can never really be too large. The more space they have, the less bored they will be, and the less damage they will do to the soil. More often than not, farmyard pigs never have sufficient room for their numbers, so they end up overgrazing and ultimately ruining the landscape.

But pigs are not alone in this matter. Millions of acres of land are overgrazed by cattle and horses because their owners simply do not manage their lands efficiently. They try to keep too much livestock on insufficient acreage and make matters worse by not caring for the grazing lands as well. If you have a very large plot that can be devoted to a paddock, it is advisable to section this such that your pet can have access to it on a rotational basis. You are not faced with the economic problems related to farming, so you can allocate as much space as possible for your pet pig.

The exotic miniature pig breeds are only about a quarter to an eighth the size of typical farm pigs, so they are unlikely to damage soil and vegetation in anything like the manner their commercial cousins will. You are unlikely to keep more than one or two as pets, so you do not actually need a vast amount of room to provide a miniature pasture. From the foregoing, you can see that it takes no more to cater to a pig, either indoors or out, than to a dog, a collection of birds, or most other popular pets.

If you intend to breed your pet, your housing accommodation should include a separate farrowing (birthing) area. It should be barricaded so that the sow cannot try to jump out and injure herself.

Feeding

Of all the pets we humans keep, I doubt there are any others that are quite so simple to feed as pigs. Goats may come very close, but one might elevate the pig into a league of its own. There is virtually nothing it will not gobble up. This may seem an ideal situation, which it is in many ways, but it can result in your pet becoming "as fat as a pig." Obesity is a major problem in pets. This is certainly true of the pot-belly if you do not carefully monitor its diet. Most pets know when they have eaten their fill, but pigs have an appetite that almost has no limits: they will often gorge well beyond the level that is good for them.

COMMERCIAL FEEDS

The basic diet of your pet should be centered around commercial pig foods. However, you do not want by preference the normal feeds given to farm pigs because they are intended to put weight on pigs at a very rapid rate—so they can be converted into pork chops and bacon at a very young age. Your pet needs to build up its weight more naturally.

Purina produces a number of special mini-pig foods that can be purchased in suitably sized bags that will last you quite a few weeks. They are fortified with minerals, including vitamin E, which is essential to these pets. They are also high in fiber content. Each of these foods is formulated to be especially beneficial to mini pigs within given age ranges. There are those for piglets under six months of age, and those for piggies over that age. Another producer of mini pig food is Heartland Exotics. Your local feed and grain merchant may not stock the full range of these foods but will be happy to order those that you want. Given the growing popularity of these little pigs, it shouldn't be too long before special mini

Opposite: To keep your pig in good physical condition, provide a good diet and avoid the feeding of junk foods.

The basic diet of the pig is fairly simple and relatively inexpensive.

The main staple of your piggie's diet should be a commercial pig food specially formulated for miniature pigs. Do not offer standard farmyard-pig food, which is formulated to fatten pigs, to your pet.

pig food will be obtainable at pet shops.

Because the various commercial feeds contain differing ratios of proteins and carbohydrates, it is not possible to quote the quantities that your pig should receive on a daily basis. The guidelines are printed on the bags and are related to the weight of your pig. As a very rough guide, a pot-belly will consume about 8 to 10 oz. of a suitable mini pig food per day. A piglet will eat less than this, so these pets are actually very economical to feed, being much less costly than the average dog.

TABLE SCRAPS

While your pet porker will happily eat any scraps you care to offer it, you must understand from the outset that this method of feeding is actually not good for the animal. Forget the fact that the pig will take scraps readily, and think more in terms of what will happen to it if it consumes too much of this sort of piggy junk food. It will rapidly become obese and may lack vital minerals and vitamins. This may result in nutritional deficiency or imbalance. The effects may be weakened leg joints and subsequent lameness, greater risk of liver and heart problems, breeding problems in sows, and arthritis even before the pet reaches old age.

You may supply your pig with limited quantities of fresh hay or long-stem alfalfa. Alternatively, pelleted hay can be given. You can also supply the animal with *small* bits of vegetables and fruits. Never feed it chocolates and other sweet items as they may badly affect its health. Treats should be in the form of raisins, carrots, bits of apple, grapes, and similar items. You must watch that the pig is not given excessive amounts of proteins; otherwise, it will gain weight too quickly. Bear in mind that the commercial feed you are supplying will already contain a 12 to 14% protein content that is formulated to meet your pig's needs of this important compound.

VITAMIN AND MINERAL SUPPLEMENTS

Much has been written about the importance of vitamins and minerals in pets, but it must be remembered that an excess is every bit as dangerous as a deficiency. Indiscriminate use of supplements is, therefore, not recommended because you cannot know whether you are guilty of overkill. Supplements of vitamin E in capsule form can, however, be recommended because those added to commercial feeds lose potency over a time period—the shelf life of the vitamin being short. Recommended amounts differ greatly, according to the person recommending them; but if you work on the basis of 50 to 100 IU (International Units) per day, you should be in the safe zone. The capsules can be fed as a treat and are available from any pharmacy. Iron and selenium deficiencies may be a problem in very young piglets; but if this is so, they should have been rectified weeks before the piglet was old enough to be sold. The best advice you can get with respect to vitamins and minerals is to let your vet advise you if any are needed. This subject can be discussed at those times your pet is receiving its injections and checkups. Of course, if you suspect a problem at any time, you should discuss the matter with your vet.

WATER

It is crucial that your pig has access to water 24 hours a day. The water should be changed daily or as often as it clearly needs to be replenished. Just by looking at a pig, you will appreciate that its body contains a large volume of liquid, so it should *never* be made to go without this elixir of life—for even short periods.

Your pig's feeding utensils should be removed and cleaned after each meal. Clean fresh water should be available at all times.

It is up to you to provide the proper amount of food to your pig. If you are not sure about the amount to feed, check with your veterinarian.

HOW OFTEN TO FEED

The main diet is best fed over two meals: one in the morning and one in the late afternoon or early evening. Your pet will fit in with your timetable, but try to offer meals on a regular schedule each day. Naturally, you can have more flexibility when it comes to treats.

OBESITY, DIET, AND ASSESSING CONDITION

No pet suffers more from obesity than a pet pig. This is because it is forever wanting more food. Given its required rations, it will still look appealingly at you when they are gone as if to say, "You are not giving me enough." It takes a very strong-willed person to resist these pets. Your guide to whether or not your porky friend is getting enough food is its condition. You should be able to feel its ribs without undue problem. If you cannot, it is eating too much. Conversely, if you can see its rib cage without the need to feel it, then your pet is definitely underfed.

Your pig should be lively, display a clear eye, and have a healthy interest in you and the world around it. If it becomes too fat, and very many do, the answer is never to put it on a short-term starvation diet. This is dangerous to its health. Commence by reducing the quantities of food being given, especially those that might be regarded as "junk." They will include high-protein or high-fat-content foods (excluding the basic commercial rations), cookies, bread, and other similar items. Your pet will not shed weight overnight, so you must stick to this regimen for many weeks and try to assess if the diet is producing results. By all means, discuss the problem with your vet.

FEEDING UTENSILS AND METHOD OF FEEDING

Even the most ardent pig fan would have to agree that these animals are not the most delicate of eaters—either in the amounts they can consume, or in the manner of their feeding.

Food bowls should be sturdy and easily cleanable. Your pet shop stocks accessory items that are suitable for your pig.

They are noisy eaters and sloppy drinkers. Their table manners will thus not impress your non-pig-owning friends! Food and water containers should be large enough for the pigs to get their snouts into and around. They should also be heavy— such as crock pots used for large dogs. You can purchase aluminum pig feeders from agricultural suppliers, but these are only worthwhile for pigs kept outdoors, and even then a single pet can be given the easy-to-clean dog bowls. If the dish is not heavy enough, your pet will delight in throwing it around the kitchen.

With regard to water, your pot-belly may be compared to a Saint Bernard dog in the amount of water that it will slurp over the edge and around its dish. As it satiates its need, it will walk away with water dripping from its jaws. I am afraid this is the way pigs are, so it is something you must accept with these little darlings! You can place the water dish in a large shallow plastic pan, which would confine some of the mess, or you can place a towel under the dish to soak up the spillage.

FORAGING, OR ROOTING, BOX

In order to make your pig work a little for its food, you could easily make a foraging, or rooting, box. This is simply a large flat box that the pig can walk into with ease. It will, of course, need sides that are high enough to prevent the contents from being rooted out of the box. You place a quantity of large pebbles in it, together with some tufts of grass or weeds, and clean soil (or just a mixture of differing sized pebbles). Scatter tidbits in the box. Porky will then delight in foraging and will thus fulfill a natural instinct to root around in the earth to find food items.

Pigs especially love watermelon rind, but if they consume it in large quantities, it can cause digestive problems. This is a food that should be offered in limited quantities—as a treat.

Care of the Pot-Bellied Pig

The way in which you should go about the business of general care for your little pig is much the same as for any other pet that is going to share your home.

The first thing you must do is to ensure that you have all of the things you are going to need in advance of the pig's arrival. This is much better than having to rush around at the last moment and maybe having to settle for items that are not quite what you want. The following list will be useful in this respect:

1. Bed or dog crate. You may have one or both of these. Remember, the bed must be durable enough to withstand the pressure of your pet's weight. A dog crate (made of strong weldwire panels) can be purchased from your pet shop. A crate can be used to transport your piggy, and it can double as a bed if it is suitably lined with paper on the bottom. Blankets are then placed on top of the paper.

A crate can be very handy on those occasions when you might wish to confine porky in the home for short periods—or when you are traveling on vacation. Do make sure it is large enough for your pet to lie stretched out in, and high enough that the animal can stand up without touching the top panel.

2. Sturdy, easy-to-clean food and water pots.

3.Bedding blankets.

4. A stock of old towels for wiping porky down if he gets wet or muddy.

5. A medium-bristle dog brush.

6. Well-fenced facilities in which your pet can play and exercise.

7. A litter tray if you plan to housebreak porky to attend to his toiletry needs indoors. A

Opposite: The notion that pigs are dirty animals is hogwash. It is based on the way humans have treated the pig, rather than on the actual qualities of the animal.

very large plastic tray will be best. The front can be cut out for easy access. You will need a quantity of clean pine, or similar wood, shavings that have not been treated with chemicals. Cat litter is not a good idea because your pet might eat some of it. Be sure to clean out the litter pan on a daily basis.

8. A harness so your pet can be trained to walk on a leash. Cotton webbing is the best material to use as nylon might create sores on the pig's body. Leather that is lined with soft material is an alternative. You can use a small-dog or -cat harness for a baby piglet until you locate a seller of pig harnesses or make your own.

9. A supply of commercial pig food. Do not purchase so much that it will be stored for months and quite possibly become spoiled.

SECURITY

Before your pig is collected, you should go around your home looking for all potential dangers to the piglet. For example, never leave any medicines where your pet might get hold of them. The same applies to cleaning materials, such as disinfectants and polishes. Paint also should be kept away from your pet. Indoor plants are yet another possible danger—some are poisonous to pets.

Wires trailing to electrical implements are an obvious danger to a little piglet, which inherits a natural curiosity to nibble on everything. Never leave an iron on its board because a piglet will just love to pull on the cord.

Needless to say, a balcony is a definite danger to a piglet, so it must be very well secured with wireweld or a similar material.

Likewise, while pigs are, in fact, excellent swimmers, a garden pond or a swimming pool is a major danger to a pig. If it should fall in, it may not be able to clamber out, so be sure to fence in pools and ponds.

Your little piggie will miss its mother and siblings when it first arrives in your home. It will need time to adjust to its new environment.

COLLECTING YOUR PET

Try to collect your piggy as early in the day as possible so that it has time to settle down and relax when it arrives in its new home. When traveling, do make a number of stops on a long journey, and have someone with you to control the pig, or transport the animal in a crate. Do not let your vehicle become too hot, and do not directly expose the piggy to a draft from open windows. Have a supply of fresh water with you so the pig can have a drink en route. Take a quantity of old toweling with you to soak up any puddles the pet may make in its crate.

ON ARRIVAL HOME

Moving out of its first home is a very traumatic experience for any animal so do not let children immediately pick up the new pet. Place it into a large puppy pen or another restricted place so it can rest from its journey. Offer it a light meal, and, of course, water.

It is best to restrict porky to a single room or two initially, such as the kitchen and main living room, so it is in a controlled environment while you house train it. According to your wishes, it can then be allowed into other rooms once it is house trained.

If it has come from home-kept stock, it will no doubt already be house trained, and you will be very glad you paid the extra cost for such a pet. It will make your job much easier than if you had to attend to this task.

HANDLING PIGS

One of the main reasons why pigs and all other pets may come to dislike being picked up is that, at some early point in their lives, they were dropped or mishandled. Children are notorious on both of these counts so it is up to you to supervise matters at all times.

Bear in mind that cats and dogs are very athletic: when dropped, they will more often than not correct the fall and land relatively safely. This is not so with a pig, which will land with an ungainly thud that could result in permanent injury.

It must be firmly, yet gently, secured with both hands and then held close to your body. You must talk soothingly to it because young piglets are very nervous and excitable critters that will wriggle frantically if they are frightened.

Again, the piglet that has come from a home environment will already be quite familiar with being handled, while those from outdoor piggeries that have been bred as investment returns will be a totally different story. They will need very careful handling during the first week or two.

THE FIRST NIGHT

Your pet will certainly miss its siblings on the first night. One little tip that might help is to place a ticking clock near its bed. This is as close as you can come to creating a heartbeat sound (like that of the mother pig) that will comfort the youngster.

The little piggy must have plenty of blankets on which to lie so that there is no risk of its becoming cold. Piglets are very similar to human babies in terms of the warmth they need.

A cuddly toy bear or similar plaything that your pet might cuddle up to may also be greatly appreciated. However, as with those produced for cats and dogs, be very sure that it is sturdy and is not the cheap kind that damages easily. Those made of plastic should be avoided.

GROOMING YOUR POT-BELLIED PIG

Any little pig that is allowed outdoors, as all pigs should be, is going to get dirty. It will enjoy rolling in soft earth, whether it be dry or a mud bath. There is no need at all to be continually bathing your pet. Indeed, this will remove its natural skin oils, few that it has.

If your pet does get muddy, the best way to clean it is to let it dry off in a good-sized box of straw or hay. It can also

Grooming can help to keep your pot-bellied pig looking his best, but it is important to remember that skin and hair condition are primarily influenced by diet.

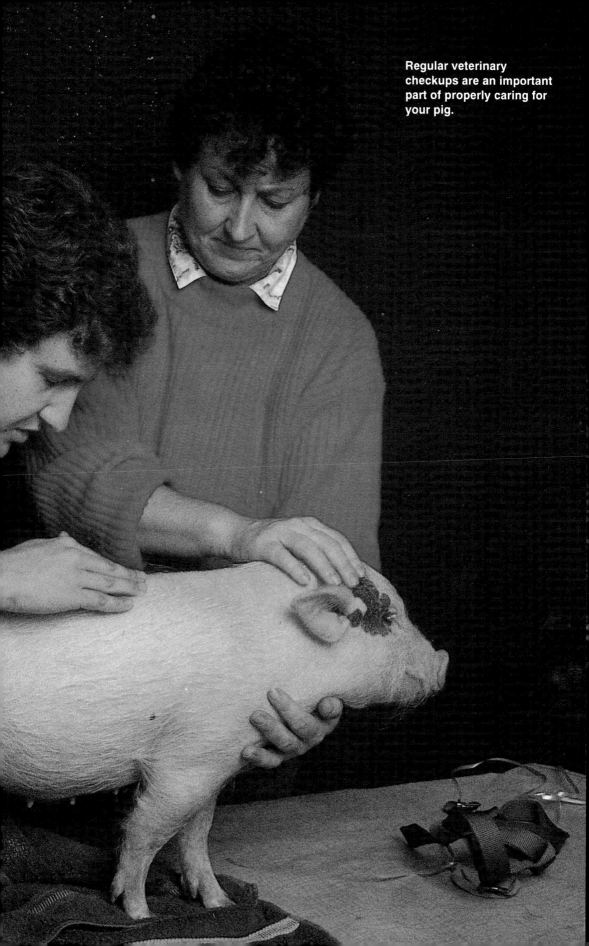

Regular veterinary checkups are an important part of properly caring for your pig.

Opposite: Brushing will remove loose hair and dried skin particles. A medium-bristle brush will work well for this purpose.

be given a toweling down. It will very quickly become clean, and in this matter is much easier to keep tidy than is the average dog or cat that has been in the rain.

If a periodic bath is necessary, this should be done in a shower stall, or in the yard if the weather is warm. The usual rules of bathing a pet should be applied.

1. Never let shampoo get into the pig's eyes: this will really put it off being bathed.

2. Never allow water to get into the pig's ears.

3. Always be sure the water temperature is warm, never too hot or ice cold.

4. Use the right shampoo—in this case, one especially formulated for pot-bellied pigs.

5. Be very sure the shampoo is thoroughly rinsed from every part of your pet or it will cause the same problems for the animal as it would to your own skin and hair.

6. Make sure the piggy has a good toweling down and is placed for at least one hour in a warm area. This will prevent the possibility of the piggy's getting chilled. In the summer months, it will dry quite nicely outdoors.

Pigs vary considerably in their attitude toward being bathed. Some really enjoy it, especially during hot weather; others merely tolerate it. Often, it is dependent on how the owner has gone about the task—whether it is a pleasurable experience or an ordeal. During very hot weather, your pot-bellied friend will enjoy splashing around in a wading pool.

Normal regular grooming will entail giving your pet a brisk brushing and a wipe with a silky cloth. You can apply hoof oil, as used for horses or cattle, to its hooves. This will keep them in really nice condition.

Some owners apply non-scented skin lotions or oil to the body of their pets; others feel that doing so isn't necessary. The problem is if the piggy goes out and has a good roll in the dirt, it will cling to the skin. Your pig is not a human

Part of the time that you spend each day with your pig should be used to observe him for any physical problems. The sooner that you detect something is wrong, the likelier it is to be remedied with no further complications.

so do not treat it as though it was. Do not apply scented products to your pet as they can create skin problems.

PHYSICAL CHECKS

At least once a week you should give your pet a physical check. Apart from the obvious benefits, this will also be good reinforcement for the pig in terms of its getting used to being handled. The ears should be inspected for evidence of ear mites. Wipe the ear with a mild solution of alcohol and water, or use a preparation from your vet. Never probe deep into the ear as this could cause damage.

Cheek the teeth to see that they appear in good shape. They can be periodically cleaned by your vet. Inspect the hooves for any signs of damage or the need to be trimmed. Again, your vet can attend to this, or perhaps show you how to go about it.

Be watchful of the eyes and any areas of excessive skin folds. While pigs do not suffer from many of the parasites that may afflict furry animals like cats, dogs, and rabbits, they can be attacked by skin mites that burrow into a fold of skin.

These mites will be more likely in breeds such as the pot-belly because pot-bellies are very prone to obesity and excessive skin folds. Any signs of parasitic invasion should be treated by your vet. Do not use remedies for dogs and cats because you will not know if you are treating for the parasite that your pet has.

You are strongly recommended to periodically let your vet give your porcine pal a look-over. This can be done each time the animal goes for its booster shots, which should not be allowed to lapse.

These periodic veterinary checkups are very important because pigs are not cats or dogs and suffer from many diseases with which you will not be familiar. Only your vet will be able to advise you on them and their treatments. If you can locate a vet in your vicinity that specializes in exotic animals, so much the better.

In the event that you run up against a problem that you do not know how to solve, then always contact the person from whom you purchased your pet. Alternatively, you may know another local pot-bellied pig owner or you can contact one of the pot-bellied associations. Apply good old common sense to general care, and you will rarely go far wrong.

IDENTIFICATION

Farmyard pigs are identified by the use of tags, which are attached to their ears. You may not wish to use them. An alternative is to have the ear tattooed. Your pig can then be registered with the appropriate pig registry service. In the event that your piggy gets lost or is stolen, its registration may be helpful in your getting the animal returned to you.

Of course, a collar with a name tag on it may be your preferred choice, but collars can get caught up on things so are not without risk.

KEEPING A PIG HEALTHY

Like any other animal, your pot-bellied pig can suffer from any of an extensive list of diseases and ailments. Some are airborne; others rely on direct contact for transmission. In many instances, dirty living conditions are the problem: colonies of pathogenic (disease-causing) bacteria build up. Minor skin abrasions caused by fighting or other injury may, in themselves, not be very serious, but they can be the site of secondary infections, which can be extremely dangerous. They give bacteria direct access to the bloodstream.

Both internal (usually worms) and external parasites can invade your pet pig. Instances of the latter are rare in pigs, due to the thickness of the skin and the sparse hair. They will usually be found on the thinner skin around the eyes and ears, as well as

In most cases, an animal that is ill will exhibit some physical sign or a change in behavior. Eating habits, in particular, can serve as a gauge of how your pet is feeling.

within the folds of skin.

If you studied the list of potential porcine diseases, it would frighten you—but this is true of any pet. For most of the major diseases, there are vaccinations to protect your pet.

Hygienic husbandry and a careful feeding regimen should minimize the other problems to the point that porky enjoys a carefree and very healthy life. For minor ailments and parasites, there are suitable medications available from your veterinarian.

HEAT AND COLD

Your little piggie is especially subject to both hypothermia and heatstroke. During the winter, it must be provided with warm accommodation; during the summer it should be kept in a cool environment. If your pet is outdoors, it must have some shade and access to a wading pool so that it can cool down. Should it ever become overheated, you must either place it into a container of cool water or place towels of cold water over its back to bring its temperature down as quickly as possible. Never leave your pig in a hot car with the windows closed.

RECOGNIZING ILL HEALTH

While it is true that any animal can contract an ailment without displaying any clinical signs, such happenings are quite rare. In most instances, your pet will show either physical signs of a problem or its behavior pattern will change, thus alerting you to the fact that something is amiss. To appreciate any abnormality, you must, of course, be aware of what normality is for your particular pet. You can only know this by constant and close contact and observation.

You will know whether or not your pig is normally a gluttonous eater, if it normally sits in this or that place, and if it is normally a very clean animal in respect to its toiletry habits. You will also know the normal state of its fecal matter. Any slight change should prompt closer study and consideration of what might have happened over the previous 48 hours. Has piggy eaten something that might not have been fresh? Has it been out in an unshaded area during a very hot day? Have any other porky-owning friends been visiting? Maybe they introduced a bacteria or virus via their clothes? Have you been to a county fair or other place where pigs may have been?

You must make notes on what prompted you to suspect that your pet is not its normal self so that when you contact your vet you can relate as much information as possible—including which vaccinations your pig has been given and whether or not they are up to date.

While pigs may have their "off" days, any minor problems, such as a chill or a stomach upset through overeating, should correct themselves within 36 hours. If they do not, you must contact your vet. Otherwise, a condition that could have easily been treated in its early stages may progress to be much more difficult (and costly).

Physical signs of illness will include: diarrhea, weeping eyes, excessively wet nose, heavy wheezing, swellings on the nose or body, problems related to breeding difficulties, and the inability of a piglet to gain weight.

Do not attempt to diagnose and treat an illness yourself. Most physical symptoms, especially diarrhea, may be indicative of any of a number of diseases that can only be identified by microscopy, blood testing, or other laboratory techniques.

GENERAL HYGIENE

If you have only a single pet pig, the chances of its contracting a major illness is dramatically reduced—compared to situations where two or more pigs are kept, or where there are farm pigs nearby. Even so, always ensure that your hygiene standards are exemplary. Never leave food bowls on the floor after meals—wash them

The outdoor areas to which your pig has access should be well maintained. Keep grass at a reasonable length, and do not accumulate piles of rotted grass clippings.

right away. Clean and replenish water bowls daily—or more often as needed. Discard and replace cracked or chipped food pots. Never feed "off" or stale food. Store all food items in a cool dry cupboard.

In outdoor locations, be sure food is not at risk from mice or rats. Wash or hose down outdoor housing at least every week and more often if it clearly needs it. Do not pile up rubbish and fecal matter in the vicinity of the pig's pen. They can be a major health hazard, as can piles of rotted grass cuttings or other vegetation.

Groom your pig regularly, and inspect its ears, eyes, teeth, hooves, and skin as a matter of course at such times. If you happen to know another pet pig owner and you know he does not maintain good health standards, you will need to brush up on how to keep him and his pet away from your piggie without offending them!

Remember that if you should visit a piggery, or a county fair where there are pigs, you could easily transport bacteria home on your clothes. Play it safe, and change when you get back home. In outdoor situations, always wear a nylon overall and rubber boots when cleaning out the pig pen. Always wash hands after handling an ill pig. If more than one porker lives in your home, try to isolate any that are ill. This is obviously crucial in a herd situation. You should erect a small quarantine pen and shelter as far away from your main stock as possible.

VACCINATIONS

Protection needed by those people with a small breeding nucleus will be much more extensive than that required by those who are simply pet owners. However, even those with a pet must consider their locality and whether or not they plan to involve themselves in the exhibition side of the hobby.

If you live in a rural district in which there are many farm pigs, you might need to vaccinate your pet against more diseases than if you live in an area with no pig population.

Before you obtain your pet, it should have received protection against leptospirosis, erysipelas, and atrophic rhinitis. The vaccines are given when the piglets are three to six weeks of age. Boosters then follow a few weeks later, thereafter either annually or biannually depending on the disease.

Breeders need to vaccinate breeding boars and sows against diseases about six weeks prior to breeding, then again three weeks later, and again before farrowing. Apart from protection against the diseases already discussed, the breeder needs to protect his stock against porcine parvovirus, *Escherichia coli*, pseudorabies, *pasteurella*, transmissible gastroenteritis, and others. Each disease does not necessitate a separate vaccination because in some instances the vaccines are combined in one injection. A breeder will need to routinely de-worm his stock prior to

breeding. Quarterly blood testing for pseudorabies and brucellosis may also be a state legal requirement.

It may seem, for a breeder in particular, that the vaccination schedules are rather involved. This is true and reflects the fact that pet pigs of any variety are subject to the same rules as commercial herds. (Pig farms are monitored on a very strict basis by the federal government because some diseases are transmissible to other farm and domestic livestock.)

A breeder who tries to evade his responsibility may be subject to a severe fine and having his stock destroyed. For these reasons, breeders should always work in close consultation with their veterinarian with respect to recommended vaccination schedules.

NEUTERING AND SPAYING

Pet pigs may well have been neutered before the owner obtains them.

Ideally, a pig will have been neutered or spayed before it goes to its new home. If not, you will have to make provision for the appropriate procedure for your pet.

Pigs require vaccinations for several kinds of swine disease. Check with your vet on this matter.

In the case of the boar, neutering (castration) is usually performed at the age of two weeks under general anesthesia. The operation is, of course, more complex with a gilt as it involves removing the ovaries. The surgery is done under anesthesia and can be performed on a piglet at about six weeks of age. However, your vet may prefer to wait somewhat longer, yet before the female has put on too much weight—which makes the surgery more complicated.

TEETH

Pigs have an adult dentition of 44 teeth; piglets have 28. The permanent teeth replace the deciduous ones between the ages of 8 to 20 months. Particular attention will be needed to the tusks, or canine teeth, which are elongate and sharp. These tusks will grow continuously throughout your pot-belly's lifetime. They will need trimming with great care because, apart from the risk of causing the pig pain,

they can become the site of disease. The teeth of the sow may only need attention every few years; but in the case of the boar, it will be more often because the teeth grow larger and at a quicker rate.

Consult your veterinarian when your pig's tusks need trimming.

PARASITES

Worms of various species can infest pot-bellied pigs, just as they can farm pigs. Fecal examination twice per year by your vet can establish the presence of these organisms. Treatment is with any of the proprietary swine wormers, such as dichlorvos. External parasites will normally be restricted to those that cause mange, which is a skin problem, and pig lice. The latter are easily eradicated with powders or lotions from your vet. Mange may be of various types. Skin scrapings will be required to determine the specific variety. Sarcoptic mange is known to be a problem

When it comes to the basics, pigs are not difficult to maintain; but they do have some special requirements, e.g., care of their tusks and hooves.

in pot-bellied pigs. It is seen in the form of bald areas of thickened skin, which may be flaky or display pruritus.

The ears are especially vulnerable to external parasites, as is the ear canal. Because many types of parasite are zoonotic (transmissible to humans), they should be treated promptly.

EYES

If your pet pig is overweight, this condition will normally be associated with excessive folds of skin around the eyes. Apart from parasitic problems, it may also exacerbate mild or full entropion: a condition in which the eyelashes turn inward onto the surface of the eye. This creates considerable irritation and discomfort and could result in blindness if the condition is not rectified. Treatment is by surgery, in which a piece of eyelid is trimmed away.

Because of the probable genetic implication of the condition, it would be most unwise to breed any sow that suffers from veterinarian-confirmed entropion. (It should be noted that a simple eyelash problem may not actually be entropion but may simply be due to overweight or other environmental factors).

HOOF CARE

The dew claws on the hooves can be kept in trim by periodic clipping with dog clippers. The large cloven hooves will require more substantial cutters, such as those used on horses. It is suggested that your vet attends to this, at least initially. Maybe he or she will show you how to go about it in the event that you plan to have a number of pigs.

As with dogs and cats, there are blood vessels running into the hoof; but as important is that, unlike in dogs, there are nerve endings that extend beyond the blood vessels (or quick). When paring hooves, it is therefore important that you take great care once a pink area is seen. Further trimming will cut into the nerve. Apart from the pain involved, this will make the pig much more unwilling to allow the procedure in the future. The hoof can be finished with a suitable file to smooth the edges.

ARTHRITIS

This condition will not be an uncommon problem as your pig gets older. As with kidney failure and heart-related problems, it will become much more likely if your pet is overweight.

Obesity has been mentioned numerous times throughout this book. Therefore, you should be alert to the fact that in pigs it really is a much more serious condition than in dogs or cats. As in humans, it is not something that happens quickly but develops over a period of time.

A warm environment can help to alleviate some of the pain in an arthritic pet, as will common remedies such as aspirin—but always consult your veterinarian first.

Pigs can be comical in their eating habits. They will stop at practically nothing to finish every last morsel.

Training Your Pig

It is most important that you train your pig to become a respectful member of the society in which it lives. If you fail to do this, it will surely become an undisciplined pet that will create so many problems for you that you may even wish you had never obtained it. The end result of this situation is that the animal will either be banished to an outdoor pen or you will try to sell or otherwise pass it off to some unsuspecting person wishing to own one of these pets. Already, I have read that some pot-bellied pig owners, unable to cope with these pets in large cities, have simply taken their pig to a park or the country and let it loose! These people, if they could be traced, should be banned for life from ever owning even a goldfish.

The subject of the training of any animal, be it a dog, cat, bird, horse, or pig is such a complex matter that a single chapter can hardly attempt to do it justice. What follows is, therefore, very much a quick review of some basic principles. Emphasis has been placed on explaining psychology, rather than on citing how this or that can be learned by porky.

If you understand the principles, you can apply them to any task or problem, rather than have a need to be told how to do this or that. It is important that you train yourself how to train your pig. If you do not understand your own failings, you are unlikely to understand those of your pet. You are strongly recommended to obtain a book devoted to animal psychology and training. Such books have not yet been written exclusively for pigs, but the principles on which any animal is trained are much the same. This so, a book on dog training is probably your wisest choice.

You may read or be

Opposite: How well—or how poorly—your piggie behaves depends on *you*. Be consistent and patient in your training program.

told that pigs cannot be trained like a dog because they are a totally different species—the latter is correct but the former is not. What you must do is to remove the specific pet concept and view training from a purely psychological viewpoint. This done, you then apply the principles to the species, taking account of any basic differences in the lifestyle of the subjects under review. Thus, there will then be seen differing motivations displayed in pigs as compared to those of a dog or a cat, but the underlying patterns of psychology are nonetheless the same. You can even apply these patterns to yourself, because you and I are as much subject to them as are our pets. Intelligence, memory, and instincts are all features that have a common evolutionary pattern.

HOW DO PIGS LEARN?

Your pet pig learns in exactly the same way as do all other creatures. It utilizes its memory and applies what it has learned to events as they occur. These new experiences are placed into its memory and create an even larger bank of information on which it can draw. The greater the number of situations it has met over its life, the greater its ability to react to situations, and the more intelligent it appears to be. However, this assumes that the way it has been taught to react has been consistent. If this is not so, it simply becomes a very confused pet—and a confused animal can be dangerous, just as a confused person can be.

INSTINCT AND MEMORY

Memory is a determinant factor in how intelligent a particular creature may be. On this basis, pigs are pretty clever animals, and so they are relatively easily trained in simple tasks. Their limitations are more a reflection of their owners' shortcomings than of their own abilities. Human failings

If used wisely, treats can help you to achieve the training goals that you have set for your pig. Offer healthy treat foods, and keep the portions small.

Reward in the form of an affectionate pat is an excellent way to reinforce your little porker's good behavior. (If he misbehaves, never strike him—scolding is sufficient.)

include lack of patience and consistency, and the tendency to misunderstand a situation. We also often attempt to apply human thinking to another animal species or to anthropomorphize their actions.

All animals react instinctively to situations. Such a response is automatic and requires no high degree of thinking. It is part of an involuntary survival strategy. If you touch a hot plate, you do not stop to ask yourself if you should move your hand away, you instinctively do this. Memory of any stimuli is passive (neutral), positive, or negative. All animals respond to stimuli in one of these three forms.

Let me give you an example. If you place a brick in front of your pig, it will inspect it, sniff it, and then store what it discovered in its mind. It will probably be a passive stimulus because a brick really is not that important to a pig. When the pig sees another brick, it will scan its memory, which will tell it that a brick is not such a big deal, so the brick will be ignored.

If you place a bunch of grapes in front of porky, it will be sniffed and the scent will create a positive stimulus. The pig will eat the grapes, and an even bigger stimulus will be stored away. The next time grapes are seen, the memory scan will again be used and the grapes gobbled up with relish. The time between seeing and eating will be minimal, due to the high positive stimulus in the memory.

If your pig happened to stand on a cattle grid and its foot slipped between the bars and caused it some pain, this would be registered in the memory as a negative stimulus. Any future encounter with a grid, or even something looking like a grid, will be avoided, due to the negative stimulus in its memory.

By this process, your pet learns about life. Now, let us complicate matters by placing a bunch of grapes on a

Training sessions should be kept short. If your pig isn't cooperating, try again later in the day or wait until the next day.

cattle grid. Now we have instinct and positive and negative reactions taking place at the same time. A pig eats out of instinct. It selects what it eats by learning what is tasty and what is not, and it modifies its instincts by scanning its memory to determine how it should react. Instinct draws it to the cattle grid, its memory telling it that grapes are delicious. But the memory of the negative stimulus of the grid tells it pain could be involved. Now its memory overrides the instinct and the pig holds back. It will pace to and fro, searching its memory for a solution.

If it is extremely hungry, it may overcome its fear of the grid and attempt to get to the grapes; but if it is already satiated, it will quickly decide the grapes are just not worth the risk. Within this example, much of what you need to know about training is embodied. Your objective in training porky is to provide your pet with memories upon which it

can draw. These will be passive, positive, or negative, depending on the response you are seeking. Where necessary, these memories will be strong enough to override or modify basic instincts.

THRESHOLDS

A threshold is the level of stimulus needed to produce a response. Pigs have a very low threshold to eating, which they will do at every opportunity. A dog has a low threshold to chasing because if it is not prepared to do this on a regular basis it would, in the wild, go very hungry. Only a few chases will result in a meal. A pig has a low threshold for running from danger. If it did not, it would not survive for long in the wild.

Let us consider thresholds in a training context. Because piggy loves food, he will go to almost any extremes to get it—with little stimulus needed. After he has gotten to the food, a mere prod is unlikely to deter him from continuing to

A pig has no concept of the past or the future. If it misbehaves, it must be disciplined when "caught in the act."

gobble up what is in front of him. A hard whack on his flanks may bring no other result than a loud squeal, and it is likely he will continue to feed.

Thresholds are thus an important part of training because differing needs by you have differing thresholds to your pet. In other words, some training goals are easier to accomplish than others. Instincts have the lowest thresholds, so it can never be a case of suppressing them but more a case of modifying them so they fit in with your needs. For example, you cannot stop your pet from urinating, but you can modify the way in which the pig goes about it. Rather than do what is natural, which is to urinate as the need is felt, your pet can be taught to go to a specific place to relieve himself.

Do understand that when you modify a behavior, your pig does not begin to understand why it should go to a certain place, only that it must because of the way such an action has been reinforced in it by repetition and a positive stimulus: praise. Check yourself when you find yourself saying, "you know you should not do that." Your pig knows nothing of the sort, and his reactions are a simple reflection of how well (or not) you have established a behavior pattern. Your pet can never be wrong because it has no concept of good or evil. Pets do not rationalize their actions or apply morality to anything. This is one of their great virtues and often one of our great weaknesses.

PIGS LIVE FOR THE MOMENT

Probably one of the most misunderstood aspects of animals is that owners do not appreciate that pets live for the moment—never for the past or for the future. This is an absolutely crucial point to remember when training your pig. It cannot relate to the past or the future, as humans can. For example, you can discipline a child for something it did a day earlier, and the child will relate that discipline to a particular event in time. Porky cannot do this. If you discipline him at the time that he commits an offense, the admonishment will be related to what is happening at that very moment. If you call your pet to you and then scold it for gobbling up the dinner that you had placed on a low table, your pet will relate your behavior to the act of coming to you when it was called. This creates what is known as the approach-avoidance conflict. Your pet wants to come to you but may have become fearful that it will be scolded for an action that it previously considered pleasurable—that of coming to you when it heard its name. This creates a dilemma for your pig and shows itself in the way the animal reacts. It approaches you and then hangs back or actually retreats. It then approaches you again and again retreats. This

response is probably seen most commonly in dogs owned by those not understanding how animals think. Often, matters are then compounded by the owner chasing the dog and spanking it for not coming when it was called. This action, which can be called a reinforcer, merely reinforces the response because the poor dog has no idea why it is being punished. The same would apply to your little porky.

There are numerous terms used to describe reinforcers in their various forms. For example, a discriminative reinforcer is any stimulus that, by implication, suggests to your pig that a primary reinforcer will be applied if the discriminative reinforcer is not heeded. The best example of a discriminative reinforcer is the word "no." It tells porky that if it does not respond as needed, a more severe form of punishment will ensue. Such a further punishment may be assumed. Thus, the pig

If you are having a problem training your pig, then it is probably something that you are doing wrong. Pigs *can* be trained successfully.

associates the word "no" with that punishment because the word was used at that time as well. Thereafter, the word "no" is all that is needed to elicit the required response. Whenever your piglet does something you do not want it to do, you should simply say "no" in a stern voice. You may also remove the pig from an "off-limits" area if that is where it has ventured. Let it see the expression on your face: animals are extremely gifted in reading facial expressions, just as we are.

Punishment, which may be limited to scolding, is a reinforcer, just as praise is. The latter is the most powerful tool a trainer has because all pets want to please their owners. This makes for a much more pleasant life for them. You can thus never overdo praise, and it should be the basis of all your training. Let us look at a typical example. If you see your piggy urinating where you do not want it to, you could, of course, simply say "no" in a firm voice. But that really doesn't achieve anything: it frightens the pig when it is doing what is wholly natural to it. It does not reinforce the desired response. Indeed, it will create confusion, and this is a negative that you do not need.

Your reaction should be to approach your pet quickly but without startling it. Lift it up, and take it to the litter tray. Praise it highly once it is in the tray. It will not immediately do as you had hoped for. If you repeat these actions every time you think it needs to relieve itself, or when you catch it in the act, it will slowly grasp the notion and will comply. Placing it into the tray is a reinforcer, as is the praise. Piggy will link the tray, the praise, and elimination as one. Thereafter, it will go to the tray of its own volition. It will eventually do this without the praise because the act itself will become what is termed an internalized reinforcer—it

Mealtime is very special for a pig. Let your pig eat undisturbed, and don't try to incorporate any rules at this time—especially when it comes to table manners!

strengthens itself every time it is done. In other words, it becomes a habit. Bear in mind that a piglet cannot control its bowel movements for more than a few seconds. Control only comes with maturation. Also, piglets will want to defecate just after sleeping, after exercising, and after eating—so these are the times to be watchful.

However, as cat owners in particular can quickly discover, this response can quickly degenerate if the litter tray is not kept clean. Most animals are very particular about cleanliness. While a pig may not be on par with a cat in this matter, it is nonetheless still less likely to use a dirty tray than a clean one. No creature likes to have to walk in its own excrement.

BAD HABITS

Pigs are not born with bad habits; they acquire them just as any other animal or human does. A bad habit is a human conception of what is and is not desirable, and we all have our own views on what is deemed undesirable. It is altogether better that bad habits are not formed in the first place, rather than having to correct them down the line. From the outset, decide what you are and are not prepared to tolerate from your pet.

For example, if it is not to be allowed into a given room, then stick to this rule. Inconsistency in your reactions creates confusion in pets. Seemingly innocent, even amusing, actions in a piglet can be a real nuisance once piggy becomes an adult. If your pet runs around the room carrying your best slippers and plays with them, this is amusing while it is a baby. But when it is an adult, you may not appreciate porky's taking your slippers, shoes and other items and then shredding them. If a piglet is allowed onto a chair while it is a youngster, it may do little damage. But when adult, its weight may result in its hooves going straight through the upholstery. If a piglet nudges you or bites your fingers, this may seem cute—but it won't be when the animal is mature!

GENERALIZATION

The problems created from that just discussed leads us to the subject of generalization. Both bad habits and good responses are subject to what is termed generalization. An example of a bad habit would be a pig that nudged its owner in order to obtain a tidbit. If that action resulted in a positive response from you, the action will generalize. The pig will nudge you any time it wants your attention. Each positive reaction from you will reinforce the action in the pig—to the point that piggy will become a pest. From a specific original action/response, porky will behave annoyingly in other situations—unless he is stopped. If your pig gets used to sitting on a chair, it will generalize to sitting on any chair, and ultimately to items such as sofas, your bed,

and so on. Only by consistent training can you limit this action to one specific chair. But it must be the same chair, of course. The same applies to nudging, if you are prepared to accept it in one situation but not in another. The word "no" can serve as a positive generalization. Initially, it is related to a specific action. Ultimately, it generalizes to any undesirable action that has no connection to the original misdeed. I would like to add another point in respect to generalization. If an animal is punished or frightened in a given environment, that fear may be transferred to any other environment that contains elements of the former place. For example, let us imagine that a pig had been punished in its pen, and later on it changes homes. It may then display a fear of any pen, which the new owner may find baffling.

However, this situation can be even more subtle: the mere sight of an element of

Pigs are more intelligent than dogs and thus can be trained more easily. If you have a pot-belly and other pets, it is possible that you can get all of them to respond to the same command, for example, "Come!"

Clara Mae getting acquainted with a Dogue de Bordeaux puppy. A dog exercise pen such as this makes an excellent temporary holding area for your pig. Piggy and puppy owned by Joann Webster.

the former pen may be enough to frighten the pig. Further, it need not be a replica of that item but can generalize to any object that only resembles it. Thus, there is no direct link between the item in the new pen to that which was in the previous one. Generalization becomes extremely complex with pets that have problems—but it works two ways. Seemingly insignificant elements that a pet associates with pleasure can generalize in the same way and console it in another environment. Identifying generalizations is thus a tricky matter of detection and testing.

COUNTER CONDITIONING

Once a bad habit has been established, there are basically three ways in which it can be corrected:

1. Punishment, which can range from the discriminative to the primary—the word "no" through to physical punishment.

2. Removal of reinforcer. This only applies in certain instances, such as when your pet rummages through a trash bin for tasty morsels, or carries shoes, or other items, away.

3. Counter conditioning, which I shall now address.

I am not sure who originally stated that "violence is the last resort of a tired mind," but this is a saying that all who attempt to train an animal should regard as a golden piece of advice. All researchers and animal trainers agree that punishment is totally unpredictable in its side effects, even if it achieves a given objective related to a single trait. It indicates that the trainer does not understand the problem, or has little patience. This established, counter conditioning is easily the most corrective tool to a trainer. It has no known side effects and relies on two simple premises. The first is that the trainer is extremely consistent in applying the correction. The

It is important that you begin training your pot-belly at an early age. Older pigs are more set in their ways and can be very resistant to your wishes.

second is to be sure to select a suitable counter action. The basis of counter conditioning is that an animal cannot be doing two totally different things at the same time.

Your pig cannot be jumping up at you at the same time that it is sitting down. Using this situation as an example, the procedure is not to reward the jumping up, which has reinforced the action in the first place, but to reward the sitting down (or standing in front of you). If, just as your pet goes to jump up at you (which is not that easy for a pig in the first place), you step backwards and say nothing, then the action of the pig will achieve nothing. The moment it stands still or sits down, you reward your pet with a tidbit or, better still, with praise and fuss. Eventually, the alternate action will be reinforced; and the former behavior, being unproductive, will be dropped. However, if you are not totally consistent in your own behavior, the bad habit will not be stopped, even though the alternate desired habit may be utilized by the pig. What happens in such an instance is that the bad habit becomes subject to what is called schedule stretching. This means the pig needs you to only praise him or accept the action one or two times, periodically—yet he will basically continue the bad-habit pattern.

PUNISHMENT AND LEARNED HELPLESSNESS

Punishment as a training or corrective means is a poor tool, especially for a pig—which is not an aggressive animal to start with. In a loving home, a light slap on the flanks may be regarded as the limits of physical punishment. But even here, the object is really to surprise the pig, or obtain its attention, rather than hurt it. Sharp words may be regarded as a form of punishment and should be effective if used correctly. Other forms of punishment, or discipline, include using a water pistol or throwing a bunch of keys or a tin can with pebbles in it (all of which are useful in situations in which you can see a wrong action but are not close enough to stop the pig from doing what it is doing). The object used may be directed at the pig's rear end or close enough to startle him. If your pet does not see you throwing the item, it will not associate it with you, but only with the action that you wish to curtail. This is important because in some instances your pet will react to the word "no" while you are present—but will continue with the wrongful action when you are away. The throwing of the item is a sort of "magical" response to the pig's action, so even if you are not present, piggy associates his action with a bunch of keys hiting him. Your presence, once the response has become reinforced, is no longer needed to illicit the desired action.

Learned helplessness is a condition created when an owner indiscriminately punishes his pet. Because the pet cannot associate the punishment with a given action, it becomes confused. It will then lose confidence in its own ability to control its own actions. In other words, it is no longer sure whether any action will or will not result in punishment. In extreme instances, the pet will urinate anywhere (rather than where it was originally taught to go), or it may become extremely timid and fearful or unpredictably aggressive. In this state, a pet is often punished even more, and the problem becomes worse—not better. It is seen especially in dogs whose owners do not have a clue as to how to train them but think they do.

In the event that you ever find that your pig has a problem, the simplest thing to do is to return to very basic training and start all over again. This is never easy, but learning must be built on trust and

Pigs that are
well trained
will not nudge
nor otherwise
annoy you
when they are
about to be
fed.

Rooting around. Young pot-bellies have higher energy and activity levels than do their adult counterparts.

success, never on confusion or fear. The key to training is by adopting the following rules:

1. Keep lessons short and enjoyable.

2. When training, never use sentences; use short phrases and speak clearly.

3. Always start a lesson by doing something the pig has already mastered. Always end a lesson in the same way.

4. Never try to teach your pet when there are distractions—be they other people, the TV, or anything else.

5. Never start a training session when you are tired or are in a bad mood.

6. If a lesson is going badly—pigs have their good and bad days as well as you and I—abandon the lesson for that day, or until later in the day. End on a good note.

7. Never try to teach a pig to perform a task that it is not physically capable of doing with comparable ease.

8. Always lavish praise for even minor success.

Never admonish failure because the pig will associate the admonishment with the very action you desire!

9. Never attempt to teach a pig difficult tasks until it is at least six months of age. However, you may teach it basics, such as walking on a lead, litter tray training, and simple commands, from the moment it arrives in your household. Just as with a child, it must learn simple things first and progress from there. If it fails to grasp basics, it will totally fail in everything else.The first and most important basic is for your pig to respond to its name and come to you with obvious pleasure—every time. It must never associate its coming to you with discipline.

10. If you are unable to correct a wrong action at the time it occurs, then shrug your shoulders and wait until the next time. You must train yourself before you can successfully hope to train an animal that does not understand the concept. An animal does

not think like you do. Its life is built around reacting to given stimuli as they happen, then recording the results—for better or worse.

11. If you are ever given advice on how you should train your pig to do this or that, or to correct a given trait, always think about it first. It should fit in with basic psychology principles, and it should not involve any form of severe punishment. If it includes the latter, it is not good advice. If you commence training your pet in a thoughtful manner from the outset, you will never experience problems. If you fail to do this, you will have problems, to a greater or lesser degree. Should they occur, always try and fathom why they have become part of the pig's behavior pattern. The answer will nearly always be human error!

If you familiarize yourself with the basic principles of animal psychology and training—about which much has been written—you will be better able to understand your pig's behavior and to train him.

Breeding

Unlike with other pets, such as dogs, cats or rabbits, keeping a pet pig in the home and breeding it just do not mix. A breeding boar will have a very strong and characteristic odor and is much more prone to moods of aggression than a neutered pig. Likewise, the unspayed sow will also be much more temperamental than will the desexed female. This means that anyone with aspirations to breed pot-bellied pigs will need to be thinking in terms of housing their pets outdoors. This does not mean such pigs cannot make fine pets but that you need to take into account their full character and accept they will not be able to live full-time in your home.

The next thing that should be said is that if you think that breeding these pets will be a sure-fire way to make a lot of money quickly, you should think again. For one thing, really sound breeding stock will be very expensive. Then there is the matter of their accommodation, which should be modern and well planned. There is no legal distinction between breeding mini pigs and those farm pigs bred commercially for their meat. This means you will need to fulfill all regulations that apply to farm livestock. You will need to comply with federal and state laws for pig management as it applies to shipping of the animals and disease prevention. In the event that an epidemic was to break out in commercial piggeries in your area, you would also be subject to any quarantine rules that were introduced. Before any piglets are sold out of state, you would have to ensure that they met vaccination and blood test regulations—for your own state and the states to which the piglets will be shipped. To all of these needs, you can add the cost of veterinary bills, stud fee for the boar (or artificial

Opposite: Breeding pot-bellied pigs requires a considerable investment of time and money as well as complete dedication to the animals' well-being. Such an undertaking must be carefully thought out beforehand.

A pregnant sow. She eventually gave birth to eleven piglets.

insemination costs), and rearing costs. Further, the mortality rate in young pigs can be quite high—much more so than in dogs or cats.

Finally, do not count on the present high prices of pot-bellied pigs to remain so. It is very probable that before you could really get underway in an established manner, your potential returns would be falling dramatically as the market evens out. Are you still sure breeding is a good idea? The average pet pig owner is, therefore, not recommended to even consider breeding these animals.

If after *careful* consideration of all of these factors you are still interested in breeding pot-bellies, then your best course of action is to have one or two pets to commence with and see how you get along with them. If after a year or so the idea of breeding them still remains strong in your mind, you will be a lot more knowledgeable about potential

problems than you are at this moment. You will have joined one of the major clubs and will have traveled about the country to shows in order to keep your eye on how costs and sales are progressing.

During this period, you can look into all of the legal requirements and plan the accommodation for your breeding operation.

GETTING UNDERWAY

All breeding must be preplanned. In the early stages, you are not advised to think in terms of owning a boar: the cost would be extremely high. In any case, you need to retain flexibility such that you can use the services of whichever established and proven boar best meets your needs. You will, therefore, invest your cash into one or more good gilts or a proven sow, which means one that has already been bred. She must, however, still be young so that she has a breeding future and can form the basis of your future herd. She must

Piglets can start to be weaned at about four to five weeks of age, but some breeders prefer to start a bit later than this...when the piglets are about seven to eight weeks old.

be registered and should be a very typical example of the breed. Try to see her parents or, at least, photos of them, and try to find out as much as possible about her siblings. Time devoted to such matters will help to ensure that you are selecting a sow that has no record of problems in her lineage. It is most important that when establishing breeding priorities, health must be at the top of the list.

BREEDING FACTS

Although a sow can become sexually mature as early as ten weeks of age, it is not recommended that a female under seven months of age be bred. The sow should be put to an established boar, never to an unproven one. Arrangements for the boar's service should be made well ahead of time; a back-up male should also be planned for, just in case there is a last-minute problem with the first choice.

The estrus cycle (the period when a female can be mated) in the pig lasts from 19 to 23 days. The pig is polyestrus, which means she will have many estrus periods during the year. They will cease only when she is mated. Ovulation occurs 35 to 45 hours after the onset of estrus. Unlike horses or sheep, pigs do not display a marked seasonal variation in their breeding cycles, though normally they may remain in estrus for longer periods during the spring and summer months.

The gestation period, the time between fertilization of an egg and the birth of piglets, ranges from 106 to 116 days. The litter size can range from 1 to 12, but 4 to 8 would be typical. The piglets are suckled for about 4 to 5 weeks, after which time they would normally be weaned onto solid foods.

ASPECTS OF BIRTH

It is not uncommon for pigs to experience birth problems. The chances of them rise dramatically if the sow is overweight. Such a female may also have

Before beginning a breeding program, you should avail yourself of books on pig breeding and pig nutrition. A knowledge of basic genetics is also advisable.

Under no circumstances should a pregnant sow be allowed to become overweight. If this happens, she may have problems giving birth.

problems lactating, so it is essential that a breeding female be maintained in very healthy condition. You are recommended to maintain contact with your vet as the sow approaches the time of parturition (the birth process).

Prior to the birth, the sow will normally prepare a nest for her offspring. She may defend it in an aggressive manner, so always treat a pregnant sow with due respect, even if she is normally placid. Many animals experience a change in their character when giving birth and must therefore be assessed on an individual basis. If the sow is denied sufficient nesting material, this may cause her to become very frustrated, which will not make her mood any better.

Breeders vary in their choice of nesting materials, among which are straw and hay (layered no more than a few inches deep), freshly fallen leaves, and coarse wood shavings. Some

breeders also like to provide the sow with pieces of clean cloth or carpeting. Your choice of nesting material will no doubt be determined by where the birth will actually take place, i.e., in your home or in a more informal setting such as a barn.

The mortality rate in piglets is potentially quite high for a number of reasons. They are very immature at birth. Unlike dogs and cats, the sow does not attend to the severing of the umbilical cord and the freeing of the baby from its fetal membrane. As a result, a weak piglet can suffocate if help is not on hand to attend to the latter process. The cord will normally sever during parturition as the piglets struggle through the birth canal.

After one or more piglets have been delivered, the sow will often stand up to urinate. When she lies down again, it is at this time that the babies can be crushed by her. Baby pigs, because of their relatively small size at birth, may not always feed well and are at risk of dying of starvation. The piglets' health can also be severely affected by a lack of warmth in the breeding quarters, a factor that must be considered in unheated outdoor pens during inclement weather. It is useful to have infrared lamps available. The period of farrowing may extend from about 45 minutes to 8 hours. The period between births can vary from a matter of minutes to about 2 to 3 hours. For all of these reasons, and the fact that piglets born last may be dead, your presence (and maybe that of the vet) is often crucial to the survival of the offspring.

BREEDING RECORDS

You are advised to keep detailed records of your breeding program as they will be invaluable to you the more established you become. As much as any other factor, they indicate to prospective buyers of your stock that you are not just breeding on a hit-or-miss basis. Records can be as complex as you wish to make them, but basic data should include the following: name of boar and sow, their age and color, when they were mated, when the sow gave birth, number of piglets (live and stillborn), how many reached weaning age, and, of course, their sex and color. Notating birth weight and subsequent gains in weight (on a weekly basis) is important. A failure to gain weight steadily over the first 4 to 5 weeks in particular could indicate a problem. Notes should be made on the feeding regimen, together with any health problems that the piglets encounter. Vaccination dates should also be recorded. Pedigrees can be filed separately, or on the reverse of the individual piglet record cards. You will need one card for the entire litter and one for each piglet.

FURTHER REFERENCES

The foregoing has been but a very brief overview of breeding, and you are recommended to seek detailed works on numerous aspects before commencing a program. In particular, you will need general pig-breeding books and those devoted to porcine nutrition. Bear in mind that the books you will find are written about commercial pig farming. Therefore, the nutritional advice will have to be modified as pot-bellies should not be fattened up like those pigs that are raised for meat purposes.

You are also advised to study basic genetics so that your breeding program can benefit from this science—both in a general way and especially if you plan to involve yourself in color breeding. You should also read as much as you can on breeding systems and on how to evaluate offspring. This will be essential in trying to upgrade your stock. Breeding is extremely rewarding in terms of personal satisfaction and may also be so from a financial standpoint. However, the various aspects discussed in this chapter should impress upon you that raising pot-bellied pigs is a lot of hard work and subject to many problems and hidden costs as well.

Associations and Registries

The California Pot-Bellied Pig Association: 1102 Aidan Avenue, Sacramento, CA 95822

The International Potbelly Pig Registry: PO Box 277, Pescadero, CA 94060

The National Committees on Potbellied Pigs: PO Box 2360 Moorpark, CA 93020

The North American Potbellied Pig Association: PO Box 90816, Austin TX 78709-0816

The Potbellied Pig Registry Service: 22819 Stanton Road, Lakeville, IN 46536

Periodicals

Pot-Bellied Pigs Magazine
SARNAN PUBLISHING
P.O. Box 853
Ooltewah, TN 37363

Glossary

Barrow: A male pig that is castrated before it reaches sexual maturity.

Boar: An intact, or unaltered, male.

Bred gilt: A female that is pregnant with her first litter.

Farrow: The process of giving birth to piglets.

Feeders: A young weaned pig that is feeding independently.

Gilt: A female pig that has never farrowed.

Hog: A swine of 120 lbs. (54.5kg) or more.

Neuter: To render a boar incapable of reproduction.

Pig: A swine under 120 lbs. (54.5kg).

Piglet: A baby pig.

Sow: A female pig that has been bred from or that is one or more years of age.

Sounder: An alternative term for a herd of pigs.

Spay: To render a female incapable of reproduction.

Suidae: A family of the order Artiodactyla.

Sus scrofa: A species of the genus *Sus*; a pig, hog, or boar.

Weaner: A piglet only recently weaned from its mother's milk.

References

Bradford, James R. 1991. Caring for pot-bellied pigs. *Veterinary Medicine*, 12:1173-1181   Canadian Council on Animal Care 1980-1984. Miniature Swine in *Guide to the Care and Use of Experimental Animals*. 2 vols., Ottawa, Ont. Vol. 2, 18:143-147

Colin, Edward C. 1956. Domesticated Animals: Pig (*Sus scrofa*) in *Elements of Genetics*, MaGraw-Hill, New York, New York 19:439-441

Garret, A.K. 1991. *Miniature Pot-Bellied Pig First Time Buyer's Guide*, JRAK Enterprises, Parker, Colorado

Hafez, E.S.E., Editor 1975. *Reproduction in Farm Animals*, Lea & Febiger, Philadelphia, Pennsylvania

Huckaby, Lisa Hall 1992. *Pot-Bellied Pigs and other Miniature Pet Pigs*, T.F.H. Publications, Inc., Neptune, New Jersey

Mull, Kayla and Blackburn, Lorrie 1989. *Pot-Bellied Pigs: Mini Pig Care & Training*, All Publishing, Orange, California

Nowak, Ronald M. 1991. Order Artiodactyla: Suidae (1336-1347) in Walker's *Mammals of the World*. Vol. 2, 5th Ed., Johns Hopkins University Press, Baltimore, Maryland

Siegmund, O.H., Editor 1973. *The Merck Veterinary Manual*, 3rd Ed., Merck & Co., Inc., Rahway, New Jersey

Pot-Bellied Pigs at a Glance

Scientific name: *Sus scrofa.*

Common name: Pot-bellied pig

Synonyms: Vietnamese pot-belly, Chinese pot-belly, Asian pot-belly
Typical height: 14-20 in.
Typical weight: 50-120 lbs. (11.4-54.5kg)

Longevity: 12-20 years

Sexual maturity: Anytime after 8-10 weeks

Preferred breeding: The female after seven months, males older

Estrus cycle: 19-23 days; polyestrus

Gestation period: 106 - 116 days

Litter size: 1-12, but 4-8 is typical

Birth weight: 4-16 oz.

Weaning: Approximately 4-5 weeks, domestic; 4-5 months, wild

Earliest purchase age: Minimum of 6 weeks advised

Chromosomes: Paired (diploid)—38

First vaccinations: 3-4 weeks, with boosters 3-4 weeks later

Rectal temperature: 103°F (39°C) +/- 0.5

Heartbeat and range: 70; 60-75 (young adults)

Dental formula: I3/3 C1/1 PM4/4 M3/3 = 22 = 1/2 jaw = 44

Index